Bed & Breakfast NORTHWEST

by Myrna Oakley

illustrated by
John Owen

Chinook Editions
Published by Chronicle Books
in association with Solstice Press

Library of Congress Cataloging in Publication Data

Oakley, Myrna.
Bed and breakfast, Northwest.

Includes index.
1. Hotels, taverns, etc.–Oregon–Directories.
2. Hotels, taverns, etc.–Washington (State)–Directories.
3. Hotels, taverns, etc.–British Columbia–Directories.
I. Title.
TX907.035 1984 647'.9479501 84-20358
ISBN O-87701-321-7

Cover photograph by Rick Semple
Illustrated by John Owen

Produced by North Country Book Express by Connie Bollinger, Karen Cathcart, and Mary Schierman under the direction of Patricia Hart and Ivar Nelson.

Chronicle Books
870 Market Street
San Francisco, California 94102

Table of Contents

Introduction

Bed and breakfast–whether it is offered in small country inns or old Victorian mansions, mountain lodges or ranches, beachside guest houses, city dwellings, or private homes–has caught on in the Northwest, and travelers want the "inside tips" about getting the most out of the bed and breakfast route.

Bed and breakfast originated in England to serve travelers touring on a limited budget. During the Depression of the 1930s "tourist homes" dotted rural and urban America offering rooms for rent in private homes, breakfast included. The concept changed and was modifed in the last fifty years as travelers became more sophisticated. Now, bed and breakfast, U.S. style, comes in several flavors. The small network of private residences offering a spare guest room or two with breakfast still exists. These regional networks are usually represented by a local reservation service. A list of these agencies in the Northwest is arranged at the end of this book.

The small city and country bed and breakfast inns, generally with less than ten tastefully decorated guest rooms, offering the travelers exceptional service in a comfortable environment, are generally operated by the owners who live near or on the premises. It is this second category of bed and breakfast accommodations that is the focus of this book.

In addition to information about the inns and their keepers, we have provided historical tidbits about the surroundings and interesting side trips to take in the region to make your stay memorable in every way.

Taking the bed and breakfast route requires a bit of an adventurous spirit and a certain amount of flexibility. When I phoned Bob and Kathryn Harrild at Haus Rohrbach in Leavenworth, Washington, Bob said, "Sure, come on over–we're finishing up painting on the second floor, so hope you won't mind a few paint cans and brushes here and there..." Later, as we sat drinking hot tea around a cheery wood stove in the European-style living room, I felt as though we'd been friends for a long time. Going bed and breakfast style is like that–personal, warm, and friendly.

A sense of humor will go a long way–you may have to share the bath down the hall, although many inns have private baths, and there may be house rules about smoking. You will probably share the breakfast table with other guests (spirited conversation is the rule rather than the exception). And for your own peace of mind, it may be best to check about pets and children–some welcome and enjoy them, others would prefer not to have "Bowser" and the four tots under the age of ten.

Brass beds and goosedown comforters, fresh flowers and gourmet breakfasts are the norm, while telephones and television in each guest room are rare. Ask the innkeeper if you need either of these amenities. Often they will be available in the common area.

There is a broad cross-section of accommodations to choose from. Innkeepers vary in their personal style from the "huggy-bear" type to the more reserved and formal host in ascot. But generally, bed and breakfast is a sociable experience and differs markedly from the hotel-motel route. No bright neon light here; rather, "come right in and make yourself at home," is the greeting most often heard by travelers.

A great advantage of staying at an inn is all the ideas you will get about the best local eateries and those special places you would miss without inside information. Innkeepers also know where the best accommodations are in the region and like to refer their exceptional guests.

As we go to press, all of the information about Northwest bed and breakfasts is current. But do not despair should you find a new proprietor–most will be able to assist you with information, reservations, and the kind of service that makes new friends. If you have a genuinely bad experience, we would appreciate a letter. Likewise, accounts of especially happy experiences will be most welcome. Drop us a line at Chinook Editions, Dept. BB, P. O. Box 9223, Moscow, Idaho 83843.

Happy traveling the bed and breakfast route through the Northwest.

Myrna L. Oakley
Spring 1984

Heading into the Sunset . . .

The Oregon Coast

The 169 miles stretching from Brookings to Florence is sometimes called Oregon's "other coast." Less peopled and less visited than some destinations to the north, this Pacific wonderland awaits discovery by those taking the bed and breakfast route.

The coastal route is easily reached via Highway 101 from northern California or Highway 199 from the Ashland-Medford-Jacksonville region of southern Oregon. Once on the route, there are several memorable bed and breakfast inns and rustic river lodges to entice you, from Brookings north to Astoria. Huge, off-shore rock formations, headlands covered by lush forests, sand dunes, rocky coves, tide pools, and driftwood-strewn beaches waylay the leisurely traveler. Take the steep paved road up to Cape Sebastian (about 20 miles north of Brookings), bearing to the left for a spectacular top-of-the-world view of the Pacific Ocean.

TU TU TUN LODGE

Rt. 1 Box 365
Gold Beach, OR 97444
Owners/Innkeepers: Dirk & Laurie VanZante
Telephone: (503) 247-6664
Rates: $70-$92

Located on the Rogue River seven miles from Gold Beach, in what some call "Zane Grey country," after the fabled writer of Westerns who loved the Rogue River. He had a cabin up-river from Gold Beach near Winkle Bar for many years, where he came to fish and write in the solitude of the rushing river and giant firs.

"Now Zane Grey's country has been invaded by the white-water rafter and the jet boat as well as the intrepid fisherperson," smile innkeepers Dirk and Laurie VanZante. "We have people who return year after year for our spring Chinook salmon run or in July and August for deep sea fishing. And other times of the year just for a little 'R & R'."

The contemporary yet rustic lodge overlooks the Rogue River on the site of an ancient Indian encampment—the Tutunis lived near the mouth of the Rogue. The river still teems with wildlife such as deer (they often browse in the nearby orchard), otter, beaver, heron, and osprey (look for the nests high atop the tree snags).

Early rising anglers at Tu Tu Tun will find their breakfast favorites and, if requested, a hearty lunch packed for the day's fishing trip on the river. Tu Tu Tun serves three meals on a reservation basis, and cost is separate from lodging.

The sixteen guest rooms, each with its own deck and view of the Rogue River, can accommodate about 40 guests and are located in a two-story addition next to the main lodge. Knotty pine ceilings, fishing paraphernalia used for decor, and fresh flowers give the rooms a touch of rustic elegance. Tu Tu Tun is a quiet, restful place, and although fishing is the number one activity, there are many other things to see and do nearby.

One of the best side trips is a 50-mile jet-boat trip up the Rogue River into the white-water heartland of the river. One of the jet boats stops at the Tu Tu Tun dock during the season; check with the VanZantes for cost and schedule. As you safely boat through the Rogue's riffles, rapids, and pools, the genial pilot points out the mud swallow and osprey nests, the blue heron, and river geology and recounts lively tales of early river life.

WEDDERBURN HOUSE BED & BREAKFAST

94361 Wedderburn Loop Road
P.O. Box 592
Wedderburn, OR 97491
Owners/Innkeepers: Ken & Lea Leonard
Telephone: (503) 247-6126
Rates: $20-$40

Wedderburn House, which dates back to the late 1890s, overlooks the Rogue River and its bridge, which funnels Oregon coast travelers along Highway 101 south to Gold Beach and Brookings or north toward Bandon and

Coos Bay. "We're a short trek from the north jetty and the beach," says Lea Leonard. "Guests like to bring binoculars for spotting seals and sea lions as well as our many shore birds."

The Leonards were intrigued with the bed and breakfast concept, and after visiting an inn in the Napa Valley, they "came home and began redecorating." One of the guest rooms on the main floor, done in maroons and pinks, has its own small sitting room with a love seat and TV. There's also a rocking chair for musing, a desk for writing or working, and a private bath.

Enjoy a glass of sherry served in antique wine glasses or sit with the Leonards in the common room for conversation by the fire. "We invite people into our home as guests," say Ken and Lea.

Continental breakfast at Wedderburn House is fresh fruit, homemade muffins or biscuits, homemade jams, and plenty of fresh coffee or tea. There is a resident canine, 12-year-old Gypsy, a German shepherd who loves people. "She's very friendly and the only danger is being licked to death."

The Leonards are Arizona snowbirds during the winter, so the season at Wedderburn House Bed and Breakfast is May 15-October 1.

For additional information contact the Gold Beach-Wedderburn Chamber of Commerce, P.O. Box 55, Gold Beach, OR 97444; (503) 247-7526.

CLIFF HARBOR GUEST HOUSE

P.O. Box 769
Bandon, OR 97411
Owners/Innkeepers: Bill & Doris Duncan
Telephone: (503) 347-3956
Rates: $45-$52

Located in Bandon, about 50 miles north of Gold Beach and Port Orford, noted for Cape Blanco, the most westward point in Oregon, Cliff Harbor Guest House overlooks a spectacular stretch of beach, including some of those craggy basaltic outcroppings and geologic remnants so characteristic of the Oregon coast.

Cliff Harbor is a contemporary beach house with a

rustic, weather-beaten look about it. First-time visitors will find it on Beach Loop Road by watching for the striking seascape mural in shades of blue on the double garage doors. You may be greeted by the Duncan's dog, Janice, on arrival, and as she wags her greeting at the door notice the unusual entry floor–slices of dark fossilized myrtlewood, beach agates, and pebbles poured into diamond-shaped concrete panels.

When Doris and Bill Duncan first started innkeeping, they rented visitors the apartment hide-away atop the garage called Cliffside Studio–complete with skylights, kitchen, and 180 degrees of Pacific Ocean beaches, with seagulls for company. The Studio has a private entrance just off the main entry hall. Two confortable double beds, a window seat with cozy pillows, and a rocking chair near the free-standing glass-enclosed fireplace will entice you to unpack with dispatch and curl up with a good book, a glass of wine, and "thou."

Each morning Doris leaves a basket of fresh-baked sweet rolls and muffins at your door, and the Cliffside Studio refrigerator will be well stocked with the makings for a light breakfast–juices and homemade jam, butter and cream, cereals (including the Duncans' favorite granola), coffee, and tea.

"We have just added a second guest room this year–the Harbor Suite," explains Doris Duncan, "and though it doesn't have the 180-degree view, you can see some of the beach and ocean to the north and it's very cozy." The folks who rent the Harbor Suite get treated to a full breakfast served at their pleasure in the main dining room, on the private deck, or in the suite. The Harbor Suite also has wheelchair access.

Take the well-worn path down to the beach and enjoy an early morning or any-time-of-day walk along the water's edge, perhaps heading north toward the historic Bandon lighthouse. Built in 1896 at a cost of about $18,000, the lighthouse was used by the Coast Guard until 1939. Somewhat worn and dejected, it sits on the North Jetty in Bullards Beach State Park, well photographed and painted by admirers all year 'round.

SPINDRIFT BED & BREAKFAST
2990 Beach Loop Road
Bandon, OR 97411
Owners/Innkeepers: Don & Robbie Smith
Telephone: (503) 347-2275
Rates: $35-$45

Perched some forty feet above a long, sandy beach, Spindrift Bed & Breakfast commands a broad view of Bandon's basaltic rock formations, or "stacks." "Great for watching sea birds, migrating whales and sea lions, and of course the magnificent sunsets," chorus the Smiths. Friendly nuzzles from Leif Ericson, resident Norwegian elkhound, add to your welcome at Spindrift B&B.

"Of course there are the seagulls, the Republicans and the Democrats I call them," chuckles Don Smith. "They seem to always congregate in two large groups, one at the north end of the beach and the others toward the south."

Don's a retired university librarian who's taken a liking to beach living, rock collecting, wine-making, and innkeeping. His wife, Robbie, an accomplished weaver, recalls, "When the youngest of our six boys left the nest I told Don 'I need something live around the house, it's too quiet!' "

Don, who looks much like New England sea captain (he was, in fact, born and raised in Maine) retorted, "Well, what am I?"

They bought the dog and decided to open their beachside home to bed and breakfast guests. Two bedrooms converted nicely to guest rooms: Seaview has floor-to-ceiling windows, fireplace, queen-size bed, and private deck overlooking the Pacific Ocean and beach; Surfsound hasn't a view of the ocean but is cozy, with twin beds.

Guests can enjoy the sunken living room with its fireplace and vaulted ceiling, and the expanse of windows allows a full view of the ever-changing sea and sky. "If you don't like the weather, just hang around for thirty minutes or so," says Don. "It's grand, this ocean where the weather begins. Although the weather can be nice off and on all year, most people like to have a windbreaker and rain gear packed, just in case of rain squalls and winter storms."

For things to see and do in the Bandon area, stop by the Visitor's Information Center in Old Town, near the Continuum Center. The Continuum Center itself is also worth a stop. It has an intriguing exhibit (originally shown at the California Museum of Science and Industry) which explores new and traditional dimensions of thought and the concept of mortality. After seeing the exhibit, you'll enjoy browsing through the adjoining bookstore with its wide selection of books and tapes ranging in subject from philosophy, science, and holistic health to contemporary cookbooks, travel, and humor. Old Town Bandon, now being renovated and refurbished by the townspeople, also has art galleries, spinning and weaving shops, and several good eateries. To sample some local products, stop in at

Cranberry Sweets (Bandon is the Cranberry Capital of Oregon) and the Bandon Cheese Factory, where you can watch the cheese-making process as well as sample the various cheeses made there.

Are you a history buff? The Coquille River Museum operated by the Bandon Historical Society is housed in the old Coast Guard building on First Street; ask about the old printing press rescued from its sandy grave on a nearby beach and brought to the museum.

For fishing visit the new Bandon harbor. Perch or rock fish can be caught off the jetty or in the surf most of the year, and crab right off the dock or by boat in the bay. Salmon and steelhead can be stalked in nearby Coquille, Sixes, and Elk rivers in season. There are also a couple of lakes close by. For additional maps and information about the Bandon area contact the Bandon Chamber of Commerce, P.O. Box 1515, Bandon, OR 97411. Telephone (503) 347-9616.

THE JOHNSON HOUSE

216 Maple Street
P.O. Box 1892
Florence, OR 97439
Owners/Innkeepers: Jayne & Ronald Fraese
Telephone: (503) 997-8000
Rates: $28-$56

Dating back to 1892 and one of the oldest houses in Florence, The Johnson House was built by Dr. O. F. Kennedy as a residence and clinic. The planed lumber and trim molding were probably brought in by ship from San Francisco, as there was no mill in Florence at the time.

After a succession of owners, the house was sold again in 1924 to M. Brody, who planned to turn it into a clam cannery. The plan was never fulfilled, however, and the house was sold to the Johnson family. Ron and Jayne Fraese purchased the house in 1981 and spent that summer doing a major restoration of the house.

The Fraeses became intrigued with the bed and breakfast concept through travels in several European countries. "We discovered that we liked the informality, the personal attention and the chance to meet other people," recall the couple. "Besides," says Ron, "the breakfast is always better."

The Johnson House is no exception. For breakfast, guests can look forward to muffins or fresh-baked breads to accompany the hearty feast of ham and eggs, fresh juices, homemade blackberry jam and lots of fresh coffee.

Black and white square tiles on the kitchen floor, white lace curtains at the tall rectangular windows and patchwork quilts on the antique beds give The Johnson House a 1920s and early 1930s feeling. A huge old Philco radio sits in the living room along with a fringed floor lamp and a pair of china poodles. A three-foot ash and oak antique clock hangs on one wall, along with old photographs and western prints collected by the Fraeses on their antique-hunting jaunts along the coast.

"Guests like to browse through the selection of books on the upstairs landing and often curl up on the living room sofa or in one of the easy chairs," says Jayne Fraese. Comfort and friendliness without a lot of frills is one way of describing The Johnson House.

The coastal town of Florence, some 60 miles into the sunset from Eugene, lies at the mouth of the wide Siuslaw River and signals the beginning of sand dunes country–53 miles extending south along the coast from Sea Lion Point to Coos Bay. Rising to heights of more than 250 feet in some places, the beige-colored dunes march with the wind, their contours sculptured by sand washed ashore and blown inland for up to two and a half miles by the westerly winds.

For a look at the ever-changing sand dunes, stop at the new Oregon Dunes Overlook a few miles south of Florence (good ramp and handicapped access). Perhaps the coast strawberry, beach pea, or seashore lupine will be in bloom; look for them on the foredunes. On the open sand can be spotted monkey flower, sandverbena, bench silver-top, and seashore lupine. Check at the Visitors Information Center in Florence on Highway 101, near Old Town, for directions. For more information about the Oregon Dunes National Recreation Area, including maps, contact: Area Ranger, ODNRA, 855 Highway Ave., Reedsport, OR 97467. Telephone: (503) 271-3611.

A short walk from The Johnson House is the Florence waterfront where, at the turn of the century, tall schooners loaded fresh salmon and small businesses served loggers, fishermen, and Oregon homesteaders. Before 1880 the area was home to the Siuslaw Indian tribe who lived along the riverbank, carving canoes from Douglas fir logs and fishing for the abundant salmon.

When you visit the refurbished and renovated Old Town area today, you'll notice antique shops and boutiques, gift shops and residences, small restaurants and coffee shops along with the small Florence fishing fleet (minus the sailing schooners of yesteryear). A comfortable and unique blend of the old and new gives visitors a feeling of what it might have been like in downtown Florence in the early 1900s.

A stop at the Siuslaw Pioneer Museum will give you a nostalgic look at logging and sailing artifacts from those early days–look for it just south of Florence on Highway 101 in the same building as the Siuslaw Art Galley. For more information about the Florence area (including the annual mid-May Rhododendron Festival), contact the Florence Area Chamber of Commerce, P.O. Box 712, Florence, OR 97439. Telephone: (503) 997-3128.

RIVERSIDE INN BED & BREAKFAST

430 South Holladay Street
Seaside, OR 97138
Owners: Stephen Tuckman & Cindy McKee
Innkeepers: Catherine & Kay Matthias
Telephone: (503) 738-8254
Rates: $29-$43

"We're offering an American hybrid of an old European custom," say husband and wife owners Stephen Tuckman and Cindy McKee. "But with more privacy. We're trying to offer an experience reminiscent of a visit to grandmother's summer cottage at the seashore, with a quiet and secluded atmosphere."

You might think that's difficult to accomplish in a downtown location, but Riverside Inn Bed & Breakfast manages it nicely. And two of the reasons are the friendly innkeepers, Catherine Matthias and her mother, Kay Matthias. Catherine's 18-year-old daughter, Lisa, also pitches in when she's not in school.

Breakfast is served in the small, cheerful library–lounge with its antique dining table, comfortable overstuffed sofa, shelves full of books, and chairs by the front window. Or, if preferred, breakfast can come to your room on a tray.

"One of the breakfast specials most people love is our homemade Pineapple Creamcheese Cake," says Catherine. "Other favorites are our strawberry butter, scones with raisins, and fruit with honey-cinnamon-yogurt." The day I visited I was treated to homemade scones, strawberry butter, and fresh coffee–delicious, needless to say.

For guest rooms, you'll have your choice of seven: three cozy rooms on the ground level, each with a private entrance, open-beam ceiling with skylights, private bath, color TV, double bed, and lots of books and green plants. In the main house are four guest rooms of varying sizes, all with private baths and some with kitchenettes. The snug attic loft on the third floor has a small kitchenette, sitting-sleeping area, and a peek at the ocean.

Wander around to the backyard for a look at Seaside's tidal river, the Necanicum, and find a comfortable spot on the lawn to sit in the sun or feed some of the resident ducks. You'll enjoy browsing through Catherine's guest scrapbook, which is chock full of things to see and do in and around Seaside, for children as well as adults. Gather mussels at Ecola Park, try surf fishing or clam digging (there's a how-to-dig-clams page in the scrapbook), explore sea life in nearby tidepools at low tide (purple chiton, spiny sea urchin, and scurrying hermit crab to name just a few tidepool residents).

Located within walking distance of practically everything in Seaside, you can stroll down nearby Broadway to the Turnaround, a concrete promontory overlooking the ocean, and perhaps continue along the two-mile promenade sidewalk separating Seaside from its wide, sandy beach.

The Turnaround represents the end of the Lewis and Clark Trail, where the party camped in 1805, nearly eighteen months after they departed from St. Louis, Missouri. Ask for directions to the reconstructed Salt Cairn where, in January of 1806, the party boiled seawater to obtain salt.

If you like live, local theater, ask what's playing at the Coaster Theatre in Cannon Beach, just a few miles south of Seaside. To contact by mail, write to Coaster Theatre, P.O. Box 643, Cannon Beach, OR 97110. Telephone: (503) 436-1242.

If you prefer your excursions to the coast to be unhurried, unharried, peaceful and quiet, it might be best to avoid the weekend of the Sand Castle Contest, held usually in mid-June at Cannon Beach. However, if you love large crowds, i.e., hundreds of sand castle sculptors plus thousands of happy, cheering spectators, then beat a path to the Seaside-Cannon Beach area–check with the Cannon Beach Chamber of Commerce for exact dates: P.O. Box 64, Cannon Beach, OR 97110. Telephone: (503) 436-2623.

Other activities available to visitors include golfing, bowling, skating, bicycling, horseback riding, and fishing in nearby lakes and streams. A favorite in late fall and early spring is whale watching, when migrating whales come surprisingly close to shore. For families with children, ask for a copy of "Kids Guide to Seaside" at the Seaside Chamber of Commerce, P.O. Box 7, Seaside, OR 97138. Telephone: (503) 738-6391.

ROSEBRIAR INN BED & BREAKFAST

636 Fourteenth Street
Astoria, OR 97103
Owners/Innkeepers: Susan Hughes, Ann Leenstra, Judith Pappendick
Telephone: (503) 325-7427
Rates: $32-$48

Located in Astoria, the oldest settlement west of the Mississipi River, Rosebriar Inn was built at the turn of the century by an Astoria banker, Frank Patton. The already large house was further enlarged in the 1950s and became a convent. In the early 1970s, the house became a home for girls.

The imposing structure looks like it belongs on the historic register–it sits on the hillside commanding a fine view of the Astoria harbor and downtown area. "We're already on the local historical register and are applying for national status," said Ann. "And the state historic preservation committee has asked to come and meet at Rosebriar Inn soon."

Guests will feel at home in the comfortable parlor, complete with leaded glass windows, original fireplace, and the homey grouping of sofa and easy chairs. "We've just uncovered the original wall treatment in the living room and stairwell–a rose-colored wallpaper with the characteristic stencil pattern bordering the top," explains Susan. "We want to restore it and leave the walls as close to the original as possible."

Notice the lovely stained glass window and original woodwork on the landing and the newel post as you climb stairs to the second-floor guest rooms. The eight restored guest rooms are decorated with soft floral wallpapers, matching towels, colorful old-fashioned pictures and prints, and either a queen or twin beds. Room One has a private bath, rooms Two through Eight have sinks and built-in wardrobes left from the convent years, and share the large bath area (three private commodes and three private showers).

Two more guest rooms with cozy sitting areas will be restored within the next year. Situated in the front of the house, they will have fine views of the Astoria harbor, where the Columbia River empties into the sea. One of the new guest rooms will have its own private balcony.

Evidence of Ann's and Sharon's collective experience in art and interior design is seen in the careful attention to detail and the loving way in which Rosebriar Inn is being restored. They're even saving a small shrine found in the yard, which will remain in the garden area.

Hungry guests will enjoy Rosebriar Inn's buffet breakfast of coddled eggs, quiche of the day, or egg strata and "Potatoes Astoria," a favorite with returning guests. Fresh brewed coffee and a selection of herb teas round out the morning repast before you venture out to explore this area of rich history.

For starters, pick up a copy of the little booklet, "A Brief History of Astoria Oregon 1811–1900," compiled and written by Vera Whitney Gault, of which the Rosebriar Inn Bed & Breakfast usually has copies available for purchase. There is also a walking guide to help acquaint visitors with about sixty of Astoria's historic homes and buildings (over 400 are listed in the historic building inventory at City Hall).

Include a visit to the Clatsop County Historical Museum on Eighth and Duane streets, housed in the elegant Victorian mansion built in 1883 by Captain George Flavel. The historical society has furnished the mansion with period furniture. Notice the six fireplaces, each with a different mantel of exotic wood such as hand-carved rosewood, mahogany, walnut, and maple. The hearth tiles were imported from Europe and Asia. It is reported that Captain Flavel was a man who liked warmth, comfort, and luxury and the Flavels brought handsome pieces of furniture and rare collections of bric-a-brac from their trips to San

Francisco, New York, and abroad to furnish and beautify the home.

For a close-up look at the winter headquarters of Lewis and Clark, find Fort Clatsop about three miles east of Highway 101 between Astoria and Warrenton. There is a living history program form June to September–including buckskin-clad park rangers, live musket firing, boat carving, tanning, and map making–all frontier skills used at Fort Clatsop during that first winter of 1805–1806. Within 25 miles are several sites described in the Lewis and Clark journals. The Fort Clatsop brochure available at the Fort will give all the details and a helpful map.

Brimming over with history, the town of Astoria grew from a small settlement to a thriving city in the late 1800s and is now the Clatsop County seat. "Don't miss seeing the Astoria Column," chorus Ann and Susan at Rosebriar Inn Bed & Breakfast. Make your way up the steep San Francisco-style streets, following signs to the 125-foot high column atop Coxcomb Hill, with its breath-taking views of the Columbia River, the Pacific Ocean, and Young's Bay. Built in 1926 by the descendants of John Jacob Astor and by the Great Northern Railroad, the murals encircling the column show scenes of notable events in Northwest history.

For helpful city maps and additional information about the Astoria area, contact the Astoria Visitors and Information Center, P. O. Box 176, Astoria, OR 97103. Telephone: (503) 325-6311.

Land of Ancient Calapooyas . . .

Willamette Valley

Where ancient Calapooya Indians roamed, gathering purple camas bulbs that bloom in early May, hunting deer and fishing mountain streams, travelers will sense the peacefulness of the broad, green Willamette Valley stretching from Salem 130 miles south to Roseburg. This gentle region, though predominately rural, is scattered with towns, hamlets, and inviting side roads that skirt Interstate 5 – enough to beckon travelers to linger for several days.

MADISON INN BED & BREAKFAST

660 S.W. Madison Street
Corvallis, OR 97330
Owners/Innkeepers: Kathryn Brandis and the Brandis children
Telephone: (503) 757-1274
Rates: $35-$45

In Corvallis, 80 miles southwest of Portland, Kathryn Brandis and her six children own and operate Madison Inn just a few blocks from the Oregon State University campus. The large five-bedroom Victorian house, built in 1901 by a local physician to house his practice, was purchased by Kathryn's grandfather. "It's been in the family ever since, serving for a number of years as an OSU fraternity house before the children and I decided to open a bed and breakfast inn," says Kathryn.

The five guest rooms are named for the Brandis children who formerly occupied them – Shannon, Honore, Katy, Paige, Matthew – Michael. "Matthew is the maintenance man and cooks breakfast once a week or so. Michael helps with weddings and has an outside job, too. Katy is our people-person. Honore, Paige, and Shannon are in college so they help out on weekends," says innkeeper-mother Kathryn Brandis.

Comfortable beds with colorful quilts, easy chairs, books, and flowers complement the roomy bedrooms, of which there are four on the second floor and one on the first floor. Baths are shared, down the hall.

Madison Inn Bed and Breakfast has two cozy lounging areas bulging with books and magazines, and the front parlor is just the place for quiet reading or conversation with other guests. The airy space at the end of the large dining room is ideal for watching TV or playing a tune on the antique upright piano.

Breakfast is a special treat: fresh juices, fruit, fresh ground coffee, a cheese strata or maybe Dutch Babies, and scones with butter and homemade preserves. "It's important to me that our guests are well-fed and comfortable," says Kathryn. "It's fun for me, too; I write notes to returning guests and pin them on their in-room bathrobes."

For additional information about annual events and what to see and do in the Corvallis area, contact the Corvallis Area Information and Visitor Center, 350 S.W. Jefferson Street, Corvallis, OR 97333. Telephone (503) 757-1505.

LILLA'S HOUSE BED & BREAKFAST

206 W. 7th Street
Albany, OR 97321
Owners: John and Mary Boock
Innkeeper: Patti Merrill
Telephone: (503) 928-9437

Patti Merrill, former bookstore owner in Albany, and her architect husband Tim transformed the 97-year-old Nebergall House (Mrs. Nebergall's first name was Lilla) into Albany's first bed and breakfast inn in December 1983, with the assistance of owners John and Mary Boock.

Albany, Corvallis, and nearby Brownsville were among Willamette Valley areas settled by members of the first wagon trains coming west in the early 1840s. From its rough log-cabin-and-shack beginnings the city of Albany now boasts one of the largest collections of Victorian houses and buildings in Oregon; some 350 can be found in the Monteith Historic Distric west of Lyon Street and in the Hackleman District to the east.

For a good overview, stop at the historic information Gazebo at Ellsworth and 8th Avenue. There's an historic tour around the end of July in Albany. In Brownsville, one of Oregon's oldest continuing community events, the Linn

County Pioneer Picnic, takes place around the third weekend in June.

For additional information (including a map showing where the old covered bridges are) contact the Albany Area Visitor Bureau, P.O. Box 548/435 W. First, Albany, OR 97321. Telephone: (503) 926-1517.

CAMPUS COTTAGE BED & BREAKFAST INN

1136 East 19th
Eugene, OR 97403
Owner/innkeeper: Ursula Bates
Telephone: (503) 342-5346
Rates: $50-$63

Eugene, located toward the southern end of the Willamette Valley, has more than a state university (University of Oregon) and some 10,000-plus avid joggers. The city's first bed and breakfast inn, Campus Cottage Bed and Breakfast, opened for business in August, 1982, and proprietress Ursula Bates has been welcoming guests to her two-guest-room, bungalow-style inn ever since.

She recalls with a smile, "After visiting inns around the state, I realized that a bed and breakfast inn didn't necessarily have to be a huge old Victorian with 15 bedrooms full of priceless antiques. I bought a vintage 1925 cottage near U of O and completely refurbished and redecorated it inside and out."

Ursula chose old-fashioned prints for the wallpaper and upholstery, paint in muted blues and soft rose, lots of green plants, some refinished antique furniture (most of which she did herself), and antique glassware and dishes for serving her full breakfast.

The two guest rooms are spacious and airy, complete with antique beds and down comforters which seem to be one of the special traditions at bed and breakfast inns. For an extra-special occasion, ask for The Suite, which has its own cozy sitting area complete with Jenny Lind bed, pillows, and giant fern, along with the comfortable queen-size bed. The private bath sports an antique claw-footed tub.

The Guestroom, with a sunny southern exposure, has an oak bed and a down-filled reading chair by the window.

The private bath has a cedar-lined shower.

The living room, with its old-fashioned fireplace and print sofa and easy chair, invites guests to toast by the fire, read, visit with other guests, or work at the house jigsaw puzzle. "On warmer days and evenings, guests like the private deck overlooking the cottage garden," says proprietress Ursula Bates. "And we have a couple of bicycles for those who want to pedal around town or over to the campus."

Hungry guests will be treated to a hearty breakfast at Campus Cottage. Try the fresh fruit compote in orange sauce with an optional topping of yogurt and cinnamon, often followed by Cottage-Baked Eggs, fast becoming a favorite of Campus Cottage guests.

GRISWOLD BED & BREAKFAST

552 West Broadway
Eugene, OR 97401
Owners/Innkeepers: Phyllis & Les Griswold
Telephone: (503) 683-6294
Rates: $35-$45

Phyllis and Les Griswold acquired their innkeeping skills early in life – they raised eight sons and one daughter. "Our house has always been full," smiles Phyllis. "Now, our guests seem more like members of the family – they usually end up eating with us at the round table in the kitchen rather than at the formal dining room table."

Breakfast is a family-style affair with waffles and scrambled eggs, or a special quiche and fresh-baked biscuits, and, "always my homemade jams and jellies – grape, apple, blackberry, strawberry."

The guest rooms, all located on the second floor, are decorated in shades of blue and peach with accents of white and pink. The handsome antique maple bedroom set in the peach room belonged to the Griswold family. Rocking chairs, reading lamps, and small baskets containing washcloths, soaps and shampoos are found in each guest room.

Downstairs is a comfortable common room with a fireplace to warm travelers on blustery evenings. Griswold Bed and Breakfast is close to jogging trails and bike paths, and is only a few blocks from downtown Eugene shops, library, and eateries.

McGILLIVRAY'S LOG HOME BED & BREAKFAST

88680 Evers Road
Elmira, OR 97437
Owners/Innkeepers: Dick & Evelyn McGillivray
Telephone: (503) 935-3564
Rates: $25-$35

Although McGillivray's Log Home is located a short distance west of Eugene off Highway 126 toward Florence, you'll feel as though you're in the forested Coast Range. Well, you are–almost.

Douglas fir trees line the gravel drive to the log home built by Dick and Evelyn McGillivray. "We owned and operated the nearby Fern Ridge Store for nine years," says Dick. "We sold the store and bought the acreage here near Elmira for retirement."

The broad front porch offers a welcome "hello" to travelers, and there is a comfortable bench for "sitting a spell," soaking up some quiet and perhaps observing the resident pheasant rooster and hen under the fir near the south side of the yard, helping themselves to the grain Dick provides for them.

The small guest room on the main floor has a polished floor of fir, lace curtains, and a king-size bed. Up the handsome log stairway, fashioned by hand by Dick and Evelyn, is a larger suite with its own sun deck, and king and twin beds–suitable for a family with children.

Breakfast, served in the dining room, is a hearty affair, especially on nippy mornings when Dick fires up the old wood stove and Evelyn makes hot cakes using the antique hot-cake griddle her mother bought from a Sears & Roebuck catalog for 29 cents some fifty years ago. It makes six at one time, no less.

There are many special handmade features at McGillivray's Log Home Bed and Breakfast, such as the "blue and buggy" pine used in the kitchen, the wooden light switch covers, the doors for every room of the house, the Midwest prairie pattern fieldstone in the living room, and the massive log beams reaching up to the rafters. All the support logs are of Douglas fir.

The comfortable living room and shelves full of books are available for guests' use. "We want people to feel at home and to enjoy staying in a real log house," say the amiable McGillivrays.

MARJON BED & BREAKFAST INN

44975 Leaburg Dam Road
Leaburg, OR 97489
Owner/Innkeeper: Margie Haas
Telephone: (503) 896-3145
Rates: $60-$80

In an elegant cedar and glass home built in 1971 along the banks of the McKenzie River, about 35 miles east of Eugene-Springfield on Highway 126, innkeeper Margie Haas welcomes bed and breakfast guests to her waterfront chalet, Marjon Bed and Breakfast Inn.

A full acre of green lawn, shady green paths along the river, and a bubbling creek will beckon you outdoors for a stroll among some 2,000 azaleas and 700 rhododendrons—now, that's some backyard! A 100-year-old gnarled apple tree guards the front entrance like a wizened emporer. "The house is located on the original Huck Finn (of Mark Twain fame) estate, and Huck Finn, Jr. lived near here," says Innkeeper Haas. "At least, all the old-timers say so!"

Two guest rooms await the road-weary traveler, each with a private bath. The Master Suite is 24-feet square, with a 7- by 12-foot bed, a sunken tub surrounded by green plants, and a view of a private oriental garden through floor to ceiling windows. Sliding glass doors open from The Master Suite onto the patio and the McKenzie River close by.

The cozy second guest room has a queen-size bed, is decorated in white and butter yellow with oriental accents, and has a commanding view of the apple tree through a large window.

The main living room has a heatherstone floor-to-ceiling fireplace, comfortable sofa grouping, and view of the river. For a close-up encounter with the McKenzie, a favorite with fisherpersons too, don life vests and borrow the inn's rubber raft for a short excursion up the river and safe float back to the dock.

If that isn't enough, ready yourself for a multi-course breakfast beginning with sculptured fresh fruit (Margie's own creation) served under individual glass domes, followed, perhaps, by an egg frittata (an Italian omelette), fresh-baked popovers with butter and preserves, fresh brewed coffee, and a selection of teas. The Raspberry Tea is especially delicious—innkeeper Haas dries her own raspberry leaves. Each month of the year she changes the decor, centerpiece, and linen on the breakfast table which looks out sliding glass doors to the river, Douglas fir trees, and garden.

For information about annual events and what to see and do in the area, contact: Eugene-Springfield Visitors Bureau, P.O. Box 16286, Eugene, OR 97440. Telephone: (503) 484-5307.

THE PRINGLE HOUSE

114 N.E. 7th Avenue
Oakland, OR 97462
Owners/Innkeepers: Jim & Demay Pringle
Telephone: (503) 459-5038
Rates: $25-$35

When Jim and Demay Pringle visited Scotland and England a few years ago they stayed in bed and breakfast homes. "They were so friendly and clean," recalls Jim Pringle. "When we began looking for a place to retire, we found ourselves in the southern Willamette Valley, looking for a place big enough to house us, the two cats Pippin and Johan, our antiques, my record collection of big-band swing, and Demay's collection of more than 800 dolls. We fell in love with the old Victorian on 7th and Locust here in Oakland and bought it in 1982."

The Pringle House doors opened to bed and breakfast guests in spring, 1984, offering two antique-filled guest rooms on the second floor; you may sleep in a bed dating back to 1850 or under a 100-year-old quilt.

Two parlors on the main floor are available to guests, filled with antique clocks, a hand-crank record player, fireplace with wingback chairs close by, a rocking chair, and vintage memorabilia from their families. It's like visiting a well-loved historic museum with an invitation to enjoy and touch everything.

"We're planning to refurbish the garden, the gazebo, and add French doors opening to an outdoor dining area," says Jim.

Breakfast is prepared in the antique-filled kitchen from which fresh juice, fresh-baked breads, sliced melon, cheese, the specialty of the day (usually an individual quiche), creme caramel, and the usual array of jams, jellies, coffees, and teas will be served at the antique dining room table.

You may be treated to a look at Demay's doll collection housed in a separate room; I especially enjoyed seeing the

Shirley Temple collection and the Teddy bears (The Raggedy Ann and Andy collection greet you in the upper hallway just outside the guest rooms). The Pringle House is a nostalgic step back in time for travelers heading into the southern tip of the Willamette Valley.

STEAMBOAT INN

Toketee Rte., Box 36
Idleyld Park, OR 97447
Owners/Innkeepers: Jim & Sharon Van Loan
Telephone: (503) 496-3495
Rates: $48 (excluding meals)

Heading east about 38 miles from Roseburg, at the southern tip of the Willamette Valley, Highway 138 meanders along the tumbling North Umpqua River, taking travelers into the foothills of the Cascade Mountains. Some 30 miles of the rushing river is reserved for fly-fishing only, and situated about halfway along the fly-angling stretch is rustic Steamboat Inn.

The eight cabins all have the best seat in the house, connected by the long deck and overlooking the North Umpqua, and you'll feel as though you could sit all afternoon soaking up the river's vigorous, yet peaceful, energy.

Western writer Zane Grey came here to fly-fish. The strong current and tricky bottom give the North Umpqua its reputation as one of the most difficult rivers in North America to fish. Bring along your fly-angling equipment and waders for a try at the big ones (sea-going steelhead trout) in Secret Pool, Kitchen Pool, Honey Creek riffles or one of the other famed fishing holes nearby.

Steamboat Inn is actually more than a bed and breakfast inn; Sharon Van Loan, an accomplished chef, offers three meals a day to guests during the season, which is spring–summer–fall. You'll sit family style along the twenty-foot long, polished pine table (sawn from a single 6-inch slab of sugar pine many years ago) or at one of the tables in the glass-enclosed sun porch overlooking the cabins and river. There are usually fresh flowers and a welcoming fire in the corner fireplace at Steamboat Inn.

"Steamboat Inn traces its roots to early 1900s North Umpqua fishing camps," recalls Jim Van Loan.

"We serve new foods all the time. It takes lots of flexibility but it's fun," adds Sharon. "Breakfast may be sour cream roll-ups, a special omelette, and Grandma's Bread baked in one-pound coffee cans." And dinner during the season is a traveler's delight, complete with candles, hors d'oeuvres, and special wines.

For additional information about what to see and do in the Oakland-Sutherlin-Roseburg area, contact the Roseburg Visitors Information Center, P.O. Box 1026, 410 S.E. Spruce, Roseburg, OR 97470. Telephone: (503) 672-2648.

Shakespeare Country . . .

Southern Oregon

Southern Oregon is a curious mixture of old ghost towns and historic landmarks combined with white-water rivers, wildlife refuges, colorful caverns, a deep crystal lake, and a national forest with one of the least-known wilderness areas. For seasoning, add a good measure of Shakespeare, a pinch of contemporary comedy and drama, and a sprinkling of traditional jazz, along with Beethoven and bluegrass under the stars.

The region's tourist activity begins in earnest in late February with the opening of the Shakespearean Festival in Ashland. The 1984-85 season lists eleven productions in three theaters (one is outdoors)–from *The Taming of the Shrew* and *Henry VIII* to *Cat on a Hot Tin Roof* and *London Assurance.* For information, contact Shakespeare Festival, P.O. Box 158, Ashland, OR 97520. Telephone (503) 482-4331.

Nearby Jacksonville, southern Oregon's Historic Landmark, welcomes music-lovers to the Peter Britt Music Festival under the stars from June through August. It includes classical, jazz, bluegrass, and dance. For information, contact Britt Festival, P.O. Box 1124, Medford, OR 97501. Telephone: (503) 773-6077.

In this southernmost region of the Beaver State, there are a plethora of bed and breakfast inns to choose from . . .

CHANTICLEER BED & BREAKFAST INN

120 Gresham Street
Ashland, OR 97520
Owners/Innkeepers: Jim & Nancy Beaver
Telephone: (503) 482-1919
Rates: $59

"Sleep dwell upon thine eyes, peace in thy breast...would I were sleep and peace, so sweet to rest!" You might find this slumber-time quotation from Romeo and Juliet and a tasty mint on your pillow at Chanticleer Bed and Breakfast Inn in Ashland–that's what I found on mine – and the goosedown comforter turned down as well.

Jim and Nancy Beaver, transplanted San Franciscans, bought the 1920 craftsman-style house and completely remodeled it in 1981 (you'll enjoy looking at the scrapbook showing the construction process from beginning to end).

The six guest rooms, each with private bath, have a fresh French-country feeling with down comforters, antique wrought iron and brass beds, tidy pastel prints, fresh flowers from the garden, French windows, scented soaps and talcums, and copies of all the current plays offered at the Shakespeare Festival. I like the two lower-floor rooms that open onto the patio – handy for afternoon reading, relaxing, sunning.

Nancy's breakfast, served in the pleasant dining room, is filling and tasty. I had fresh fruit compote, shirred eggs baked in cream, and blueberry muffins. The common room, with its open-hearth fireplace, has comfortable sitting places and lots of books and games. Theater-goers often congregate here for an informal discussion over a glass of sherry poured by genial host Jim Beaver.

THE IRIS INN

59 Manzanita Street
Ashland, OR 97520
Owners/Innkeepers: Vicki & John Lamb
Telephone: (503) 488-2286
Rates: $40-$45

A restored turn-of-the century home dating back to 1906, Iris Inn Bed and Breakfast is opening its stained-glass front door to bed and breakfast travelers for the first season in June, 1984.

Offering four comfortable guest rooms with shared baths on the second floor, innkeepers Vicki and John Lamb operate the Iris Inn from mid-May to the end of September.

Notice Vicki's collection of bells in the guests' common room. "The crystal bell was used by my grandmother during Bridge games to signal a change of tables," she recalls. "And the old typewriter [a vintage Remington] on the entry table has been in the family for many years." In the same glass-fronted cabinet as the bells are a set of metal Christmas ornaments and an old wrinkled shoe Vicki uncovered when restoring another old Victorian.

For the adventurous, Vicki can advise travelers about rafting on nearby rivers–she's a former river guide.

Stained Glass Window
Iris Inn, Ashland Or.

McCALL HOUSE BED & BREAKFAST

153 Oak Street
Ashland, OR 97520
Owner/Innkeeper: Phyllis Courtney
Telephone: (503) 482-9296
Rates: $48-$53

According to newspaper clippings dating back to 1883, the grand Italianate Victorian built for pioneer businessman John Marshall McCall and his family was the talk of the town. Innkeeper Phyllis Courtney is busy gathering research on the McCalls (they came west from Pennsylvania) and the house. "I want to write down the story of the 19th century pioneer. He ran a mercantile here in southern Oregon," says Phyllis.

Notice the high ceilings, the grand, carved archways into

both parlors off the main entry hall. Though formal in design, the living room decor is warm and inviting, with lots of books, magazines, a grand piano in the second parlor, and comfortable places to curl up with a good book or converse with other guests.

There are five guest rooms with shared baths to choose from on the second floor, and soon there will be a sixth, a sun room with windows overlooking the low hills to the east that should be very snug and cheerful.

Phyllis prepares a sumptuous breakfast in her huge antique-filled kitchen and serves it in the formal dining room at three round flower-decked tables. In the McCall House Bed and Breakfast, you'll feel a bit like a wealthy Victorian lady or gentleman.

THE MINERS ADDITION

737 Siskiyou Blvd.
Ashland, OR 97520
Owner/Innkeeper: Carolyn Morris
Telephone: (503) 482-0562
Rates: $40-$50

Carolyn Morris is my idea of a perfect innkeeper. She welcomes guests into her pleasant two-guestroom inn near Southern Oregon State College with one of the most genuine, cheerful smiles you've seen, and in five minutes you'll feel as though you've found a long-lost cousin or favorite aunt.

Her interest in the early mining days of southern Oregon and of Colorado (her former home) is reflected in the old metal ore car in the side yard and in the miner's pick and shovel etched in the glass of the front door. You'll notice old maps of Oregon and the Northwest framed in the upstairs hallways and another pick and shovel window at the top of the stairs leading to the two guest rooms.

Patchwork quilts, rocking chairs, reading lamps, and old-fashioned rag rugs give the guest rooms an informal, country feeling. Each room has a private bath with a common shower.

The common room, downstairs, is inviting in shades of rich green with pale peach accents. "For breakfast I like to serve hot cakes with sour-cream-peach preserve and sour-cream-strawberry preserve toppings, and sometimes I like to surprise my guests with an old miner's favorite–fried corn meal mush," smiles Carolyn. "Guests get into these magnificent discussions at breakfast–I love seeing the interaction that happens between people. It's absolutely marvelous how much they find in common with one another–I can hardly stand to stay in the kitchen."

THE MORICAL HOUSE

668 North Main Street
Ashland, OR 97520
Owners/Innkeepers: Joe & Phyllis Morical
Telephone: (503) 482-2254
Rates: $48-$59

Located close to downtown Ashland, The Morical House is a bed and breakfast inn restored from an old home dating back to the 1880s. Innkeeper Joe Morical was tending the acre of lawn surrounded by more than a hundred varieties of trees, shrubs, and flowers on the day I arrived. Dressed in a blue jogging suit and looking more like an avid outdoors person than an innkeeper, he waved a friendly hand and gave me a royal tour of the inn.

"I was born and raised in Chelan, Washington, and Phyllis is from Ohio," said Joe as we stood in the sun porch, where breakfast is served on warm, sunny mornings, looking out on the spacious lawn and Cascade Mountains to the east. "We got tired of our California government jobs and, after visiting a number of cities, decided to open the bed and breakfast here in Ashland." Ashland is becoming the mecca for bed and breakfast inns in Oregon, primarily because of the long Shakespeare Festival season, and it's best to call in advance for reservations because most of the bed and breakfast inns are heavily booked during the summer season.

At the Morical House, visitors have a choice of six guest rooms, all filled with antiques and homemade comforters, each with a private bath. You might enjoy the lavender and green room on the top floor, "a special honeymoon and anniversary nest," says Phyllis, who supervised the decorating of the inn. "Be sure and notice the old oak organ in the sitting room–how about an old-fashioned sing-along?"

the Morial House

NEIL CREEK HOUSE

341 Mowetza Drive
Ashland, OR 97520
Owners/Innkeepers: Edith & Thomas Heumann
Telephone: (503) 482-1334
Rates: $65 (two night minimum)

Originally from Germany, Edith was a college language teacher and Thomas is a semi-retired engineer. The day I arrived, Thomas was engineering the repair of the swimming pool lining. "Some animal critter fell in and clawed its way out," he surmised.

Although the rambling ranch-style home is several miles out of town, it's worth the trip. There's a sense of restfulness and a pastoral serenity about Neil Creek House Bed and Breakfast. Ducks paddle on the pond, a rowboat bobs at its mooring on the pier nearby, Neil Creek bubbles below the wood deck, and the Siskiyou Pass mountains are not far in the distance.

Filled with a comfortable sofa and easy chairs, the large common room has an enormous natural stone fireplace, a collection of classical records, and the works of Shakespeare in both English and German.

The Heumanns offer two guest rooms with private baths – one with a canopied queen-size bed, the other with a double bed with its own private patio. Guests enjoy a full breakfast of bacon and sausage from a nearby farm, ranch-fresh brown eggs, homemade jam and syrup to go with sourdough pancakes, crepes, or Ebelskievers (like an apple fritter). It's the kind of breakfast that bed and breakfast innkeepers are known for.

ROMEO INN

295 Idaho Street
Ashland, OR 97520
Owners/Innkeepers: Anthony & Patricia Romeo
Telephone: (503) 488-0884
Rates: $63

Retired airline pilot Tony Romeo and his wife Pat moved to Ashland several years ago and fell in love with a 50-year-old Cape Cod-style house in a quiet Ashland neighborhood, a short distance from the Shakespeare Festival theaters, downtown shops, and eateries. "A builder who owned the house added two large wings to the original Cape Cod," recalls Tony. "When we bought the home we decorated and furnished four guest rooms with private baths."

The guest rooms are large (all have king-size beds) and contain welcome extras such as robes, magazines, reading lamps, window seats, and hot water bottles. "Believe it or not, guests really do enjoy the hot water bottles," smiles Patty Romeo.

Romeo Inn is one of those bed and breakfast inns offering more than the comforts of home, including a swimming pool, patio, and whirlpool spa just a few steps through French doors from the spacious living room.

"We serve a full breakfast, featuring fresh baked bagels, croissants, cinnamon rolls, muffins, or coffeecakes," says Patty. "And we offer a special cooking school each spring, usually in May." Last year the school included a class in chocolate taught by their daughter, Julia Romeo Farrell, pastry chef at a Seattle hotel.

WINCHESTER INN

35 South Second Street
Ashland, OR 97520
Owners/Innkeepers: Michael & Laurie Gibbs
Pat and Coleen Gibbs
Telephone: (503) 488-1113
Rates: $67

The Winchester Inn is the only bed and breakfast in Ashland with a full restaurant, serving both lunch and dinner, which is open to the public as well as to guests. The gourmet breakfast is served to guests on the patio or in the pleasant dining room overlooking colorful tiered gardens in the side yard.

Beginning as a private home in the 1880s, the ornate Queen Anne style structure later became southern Oregon's first hospital and after that, a boarding house.

Impressive front doors open onto pale blue carpeting throughout the inn. Each of the seven guest rooms is decorated in a different pastel–blue, peach, soft green, light brown, raspberry–with matching print comforters, overstuffed chairs, plants, and flowers.

Bed and breakfast travelers who stay at the Winchester Inn will have an easy walk to the Festival theaters, downtown shops, and Lithia Park. Be sure and taste the mineral water from the several fountains placed throughout the park, for which the park is famous.

"Shall I not take mine ease in mine inn?" queries Falstaff in *Henry IV*. Other Ashland inns offering the bard as well as bed and breakfast include . . .

ASHLAND GUEST VILLA

634 Iowa Street
Ashland, OR 97520
Owner/Innkeeper: Zelma Lamb
Telephone: (503) 488-1508
Rates: $45-$55

Among the first of Ashland's bed and breakfast inns to open in the early 1980s, Ashland Guest Villa is a modern split-level on a quiet street. It has a large yard dotted with laurel and cherry trees and a 100-foot deck facing the secluded backyard. Breakfast, which is enormous, is a grand affair, with Mrs. Lamb orchestrating lively conversation among her guests. Zelma Lamb came to Ashland in the mid-1940s from Mississippi and still retains both her southern accent and her southern charm. She'll remind you of a favorite great-aunt or special grandmother.

COACH HOUSE INN

70 Coolidge Street
Ashland, OR 97520
Owners/Innkeepers: Pamela & Jack Evans
Telephone: (503) 482-2257
Rates: $39

The bright blue farmhouse was built in the 1890s. The pear and almond trees in the yard are remnants of an original orchard. Coach House Inn has three guest rooms with shared baths, a two-night minimum stay, and a hearty continental breakfast. Pamela and Jack may be able to give you ideas about southern Oregon attractions to add to your itinerary, including the Oregon Caves.

COUNTRY WALRUS

2785 East Main Street
Ashland, OR 97520
Owner/Innkeeper: Emma Anderson
Telephone: (503) 488-1134
Rates: $45

A comfortable 1886 farmhouse with two guest rooms and shared baths, the Country Walrus has a cozy library with a fireplace for guests' use. A grand staircase leads down to the open dining room, which has its own fireplace. You'll enjoy watching Emma cook up Scandinavian apple fritters for breakfast. Take a peek through the pass-through from the dining room and notice the special honeys, preserves, and natural foods on the open kitchen shelves.

EDINBURGH LODGE

586 E. Main Street
Ashland, OR 97520
Owners/Innkeepers: Lawrence & Lynda Thirlwall
Telephone: (503) 488-1050
Rates: $56

"Our guest house, circa 1910, was a boarding house for teachers and railroad workers during the early 1900s," say the Thirlwalls. Edinburgh Lodge offers six small guest rooms with homemade quilts and private baths, each named for a Scottish castle. It is one of Ashland's most European-style bed and breakfast inns. There's a two-night minimum stay on weekends.

HERSEY HOUSE

451 N. Main Street
Ashland, OR 97520
Owners/Innkeepers: Lynn Savage & Gail Orell
Telephone: (503) 482-4563
Rates: $58

Lynn and Gail, who are sisters, have coordinated the renovation of a large turn-of-the-century Victorian farmhouse. Guests select from four individually decorated guest rooms with private baths in apricot, plum, yellow, and white. The yellow "sunshine" room has its own balcony. "Our breakfast specialties include gingerbread pancakes and eggs à la Hersey (stuffed eggs in a cream sauce with cheese)," explains Gail.

MAIN STREET INN

142 N. Main Street
Ashland, OR 97520
Owner/Innkeeper: Roanne Lyall
Telephone: (503) 488-0969
Rates: $52

This ornate Victorian dating to 1883 has three guest rooms–one with a deck, another with a small balcony, all with private bath (one is down the hall)–decorated with period furnishings. It is the small touches, the bouquet of fresh flowers and the crystal decanter set in each room, that give Main Street Inn a personal charm.

PARKSIDE BED & BREAKFAST

171 Granite Street
Ashland, OR 97520
Innkeeper: Susan Reid
Telephone: (503) 482-2320
Rates: $32-$40

Sporting a 1940s vacation house decor, Parkside Bed and Breakfast isn't fancy, but it is handy to the Festival theaters and just across the street from Lithia Park. The cottage has its own kitchen.

THE ROYAL CARTER HOUSE

514 Siskiyou Blvd.
Ashland, OR 97520
Owners/Innkeepers: Alyce & Roy Levy
Telephone: (503) 482-5623
Rates: $55-$60

The Levys bring guests British bed and breakfast tradition in a circa 1909 home, which has a secluded deck overlooking a well-manicured, flower-filled yard. There are two large guest rooms with large private baths. Try the cheerful Calico Corner room or the more ornate and dramatic Victorian Glory room; each has its own sitting-room. A light breakfast is served in the traditional dining room or patio garden.

THE STONE HOUSE

80 Hargadine Street
Ashland, OR 97520
Owners/Innkeepers: Philip & Sharon Thormahlen
Telephone: (503) 482-9233
Rates: $25-$35

Directly across the street from the Angus Bowmer Theater (indoor) and the outdoor Elizabethan Theatre, The Stone House may be one of the best bargains in downtown Ashland. There is a large basement suite with kitchen, a second tiny guest room (big enough for a brass double bed), and a third loft suite in the carriage house with a kitchenette. All have private baths. Comfortable, with contemporary furnishings and green plants, The Stone House is open during Festival season. Guests arrange for their own breakfasts at The Stone House.

WISTERIA HOUSE

453 Allison Street
Ashland, OR 97520
Owners/Innkeepers: Victor & Nancy Wigginton
Telephone: (503) 488-2302
Rates: $37-$50

Wisteria House is a comfortable family home, circa 1910, with two guest rooms, including a two-room suite, located just a few blocks from the Festival theatres. Family antiques, a sunny deck overlooking the city that serves as breakfast place on warm mornings, and squeaky-clean rooms best describe Wisteria House. You'll enjoy a continental breakfast of fresh fruit and juices, and warm breakfast breads served with Oregon jams and jellies. The living room has an old Victrola and a library full of classics. "We offer old-fashioned Oregon hospitality," say the Wiggintons.

THE WOODS HOUSE BED & BREAKFAST

333 N. Main Street
Ashland, OR 97520
Owners/Innkeepers: Janice & Allan Pinkul
Telephone: (503) 488-1598
Rates: $48-$58

One of Ashland's newest bed and breakfast inns, The Woods House Bed and Breakfast is a 1908 bungalow with a detached carriage house that was home to Dr. and Mrs. Woods and four sons for almost 40 years. "Third and fourth generation family members still live in the area," say the Pinkuls.

The rose garden and grape arbor in the backyard are being restored and can be enjoyed from the patio or path through the arbor. There are four guest rooms in the main house and the carriage house suite can sleep six. All rooms have private baths. "We can also accommodate up to sixteen for seminars or reunions," adds Janice.

Hearty family-style breakfasts are served in the dining room. Children over twelve are welcome. Look for the colorful baskets of flowers hanging from The Woods House sign on Main Street just north of downtown.

For more information about what to see and do in the Ashland area, contact Ashland Visitors Information Center, P.O. Box 606, Ashland, OR 97520. Telephone: (503) 482-3486. For nearby Medford, contact Greater Medford Visitors Bureau, 304 South Central, Medford, OR 97501. Telephone: (503) 772-6293.

In historic Jacksonville, about 15 miles west of the Ashland-Medford area, step back into the Gold Rush era. The clump of miner's boots, the crunch of wagon wheels pulled by mules or horses, the laughter of saloon and dance hall queens, and perhaps a gunshot or two seem to echo here and there through rusted hinges, around the old iron water pump beside historic Beekman Bank, and around the railway depot, circa 1891, which now houses the Jacksonville Visitors Information Center.

The courthouse, built in 1883 when Jacksonville was the county seat, is now a museum that houses Peter Britt's photography equipment and old photos and other early memorabilia. On California Street is the U.S. Hotel; President Rutherford B. Hayes was one of its first guests. Some old buildings house specialty shops and eateries, and many vintage homes on the Historic Register are still occupied. Jacksonville is a great place for a walking tour.

THE FARMHOUSE BED & BREAKFAST

755 East California Street
Jacksonville, OR 97530
Owners/Innkeepers: Tom & Cindy Parks
Telephone: (503) 899-8963
Rates: $35-$40

When you visit the Farmhouse Bed and Breakfast, ask Cindy and Tom Parks if the berries are ripe. "We often serve fresh berries from the garden with our family-style breakfast," says Cindy, "as well as home-baked goodies like cinnamon rolls, muffins, or coffeecake."

Constructed in 1929, the two-story Dutch Colonial is the home of the Parks family. Tom is a former Jacksonville mayor and berry gardener.

There are two comfortable guest rooms: the one on the main floor has a double bed, private bath, and a reading lamp and overstuffed easy chair by the sunny windows, also lots of family antiques and green plants; a large, sunny suite on the second floor is suitable for a family with children. If you need work space, there's a large desk as well as a rocking chair for cogitating. The panoramic view of the Rogue Valley from this suite is especially colorful when spring blossoms forth in the surrounding valley.

JUDGE TOUVELLE HOUSE

455 N. Oregon Street
P.O. Box 155
Jacksonville, OR 97530
Owners/Innkeepers: Verona & Nick Clark
Telephone: (503) 899-8223
Rates: $45-$55

"Schnickle" won't be living at the Judge Touvelle House anymore. Tony and Verne Beebe, who bought the crumbling, run-down house in 1981 and spent a year restoring it will be moving along with Schnickle, the family dachshund, to the schoolhouse down the street.

They recently sold the Judge Touvelle House to the Nick Clark family who plan to continue the bed and breakfast inn operation begun by Tony and Verne in 1982. The Clarks plan to open their doors to bed and breakfast travelers in September, 1984, with three antique-filled guest rooms (one with private bath; the other two share a bath).

"We'll serve a full breakfast, including local fruits and berries," says Verona. Nick is the new development director for the Southern Oregon Historical Society based in Jacksonville. Ask him about the new "living history" programs planned for the historic Beekman House and the Hanley farm just north of town.

The Judge Touvelle House, built in 1855, has an interesting history. The southern Oregon judge lived in the house from 1916 until his death in 1956. When Mrs. Touvelle passed away in 1934, her room on the second floor was closed off with everything intact, including her clothes hanging in the closet.

The room, now one of the large guest rooms, remained closed until an auction 24 years later, in 1958. Visit the Jacksonville Museum, a short walk away, for a look at more history of the house and of Judge Touvelle, who presided in the famous trial of the DeAutremont brothers who held up a "Gold Special" Southern Pacific train in 1923.

LIVINGSTON MANSION BED & BREAKFAST INN

4132 Livingston Road
P.O. Box 1476
Jacksonville, OR 97530
Owners/Innkeepers: Sherry & Wally Lossing
Telephone: (503) 899-7107
Rates: $65-$75

Sherry Lossing is one of those huggable innkeepers whose warm hospitality makes one feel immediately at home. "Wally and I like people, and this is a happy inn," says Sherry. "Even when he's gone on business trips, I manage to get the firewood in, the breakfast cookies made, and a hundred other chores done. We really believe in bed and breakfast, and to do it right, you're up early, to bed late, and you go like a house afire in between," she says. Just this summer the dining room was remodeled with a new archway entrance, and two additional guest rooms were remodeled and decorated.

There are five guest rooms on the second floor and one on the main floor of the rambling mansion. The Regal Room has its own fireplace, sofas, and wide bay windows looking east to the Rogue Valley and Cascade Mountains beyond–the morning sunrises are well worth getting up for. All of the guest rooms have cozy down comforters, flowers, antiques, and those special touches that make traveling a memorable experience.

On warm mornings you might have breakfast poolside on the patio. Sherry's breakfast cookies, usually the first course, are crammed with nuts, granola, raisins, wheat flour, and spices. Followed by juice, fresh fruit, special egg dishes, rolls, coffee, and teas. "Our guests go away full," she admits.

Livingston Mansion is perched on a hill of towering old oaks and madrona about a mile from town. Lavender wisteria drapes the swimming-pool side of the house that faces the morning sun, and old-fashioned wax myrtle with its purple flowers hugs stone steps down to the duck pond, below.

The house was built in 1915 for orchardist Charles O'Conner, then sold to World War I hero and artist, Major Archibald Livingston, whose family lived here for 43 years. "By the way," say Sherry and Wally, "families with

McCully House Inn – Jacksonville Oregon

children are welcome at Livingston Mansion Bed and Breakfast Inn."

McCULLY HOUSE INN

240 E. California Street
P.O. Box 387
Jacksonville, OR 97530
Owners/Innkeepers: Fran & Mark Dennett
Telephone: (503) 899-1942
Rates: $48-$68

The historic McCully House, one of Jacksonville's first six dwellings, was completed in 1861 and is easily found at the east end of California Street, the town's main thoroughfare. Although it was built by John W. McCully, a physician and real estate speculator, he became burdened with debts and left town, leaving Jane McCully with three children to support.

"Jane must have been a spunky lady," surmises Fran Dennett. "Not only did she become the town's first school teacher, but she may have spawned the first bed and breakfast in southern Oregon–she turned the McCully House into a boarding house." The *Oregon Sentinel* newspaper reported in 1862:

> Amos E. Rogers has taken Mrs. J.W. McCully's new dwelling on California Street for the above purpose [boarding house] . . . his table will be furnished with the best market affords and gotten up in Apple-pie order. Cost $7.00/week or .50 for a single call."

The stately old house, with its white-columned front porch and formal paneled front door, is Classic Revival in design. "We liked the polished hardwood floors and were pleased to have so many of the original McCully pieces of furniture stay with the house," says Fran.

Take a look at the square grand piano in the informal parlor. It was shipped around the Horn for the McCullys. The massive Renaissance Revival bedroom set of solid black walnut is part of The McCully Room, one of the four guest rooms. The two framed photographs over the mantle in the same guest room are of Jane McCully and her daughter, "Issie."

When I asked Fran if there was a picture of Dr. McCully, she said, "There may be one but it won't be in this house!" The errant Dr. McCully never returned to Jacksonville and is the only member of the family not buried in the Pioneer Cemetery (another interesting stop), just outside of town.

Children are welcome at the McCully House, and guests will be served a hearty breakfast in the dining room at cozy round tables. Baked Eggs Angela, McCully House apple bran muffins, fresh fruit, and individual loaves of wheat bread is a typical menu. Fran grinds her own coffee, fresh each morning. "The only problem is getting people to leave," she smiles. I can understand why.

For more information about what to see and do in Jacksonville, contact the Jacksonville Visitors Information Center, P.O. Box 33, Jacksonville, OR 97530. Telephone (503) 899-8118.

From Portland Upriver . . .

The Columbia Gorge

Portland, located on both sides of the broad Willamette River, spreads east toward 11,000-foot snow-capped Mount Hood and west into the Tualatin Valley and lower coastal range mountains. The Willamette flows into the Columbia River a few miles north of downtown.

Portland, in the 1840s, was the terminus of the Oregon Trail, and from here settlers spread west toward the mountains and south into the Willamette Valley.

Early Portlanders–whose city was named by the toss of a coin; "Boston" lost–chopped down heavily-timbered forests along the Willamette River, built cabins, and started businesses. Tree stumps were whitewashed to prevent stumbling after dark, and the nickname "Stumptown" emerged.

The stumps are long gone and in their place are broad avenues, bridges, malls, shops, fountains, parks, golf courses, and rose gardens.

Most of Historic Portland, or Old Town, is to the north of Skidmore Fountain and Burnside Street. Made up of renovated buildings dating back three and four generations, Old Town has metamorphosed into specialty shops, boutiques and interesting restaurants.

CORBETT HOUSE BED & BREAKFAST

7533 S.W. Corbett Avenue
Portland, OR 97219
Owner/Innkeeper: Sylvia Malagamba
Telephone: (503) 245-2580
Rates: $30-$45

Corbett House Bed and Breakfast is one of the few independent inns in the Portland area (there are, however, many bed and breakfast homes available through local private reservation services; see page 132 for listings), and Sylvia Malagamba is enjoying her role as innkeeper-hostess.

"I've lived on both the East Coast and the West Coast," explains Sylvia. "I wanted roots, and I wanted them somewhere other than upper New York state. I chose Portland because I'd much rather have rain than 186 inches of snow in one winter."

Perhaps that accounts for the relaxed ambience at Corbett House Bed and Breakfast and why Sylvia is tuned in to the needs of travelers. One of her guest rooms (all of which are on the second floor), The Oasis Room, has corner window views of Mount St. Helens and the Willamette River, green plants, a comfortable safari chair and bentwood rocker, and its own private balcony.

Breakfast is sometimes "whim de jour," laughs Sylvia. "Recently I found some gooseberries which were too tart, so I pureed them and folded in meringue and whipped cream. My guests asked what it was and I said 'Gooseberry Gamble–I'm gambling that you'll like it!' "

Favorites at Corbett House are Sylvia's fruit breads and her scones (bursting with currants and orange peel, and flavored with cardamom). "They taste a little like Halloween," she says. Often she'll whip up blintzes or Eggs McCorbett and bring out the homemade berry syrups.

For travelers who want to get the kinks out, there's a jogging track at Willamette Park, five blocks down the hill. Corbett House, in southwest Portland, is a short distance from Washington Park, where the International Rose Test Gardens are located; the roses are in bloom May through September. Near the test gardens is the secluded Japanese Garden. Well worth a visit, it is actually five gardens in one–Sand and Stone, Moss, Strolling Pond, Tea, and Flat gardens. It is a visual masterpiece; I always come away rejuvenated when I visit the Japanese Garden.

GARDEN HOUSE BED & BREAKFAST

2131 N.E. Siskiyou Street
Portland, OR 97212
Owner/Innkeeper: Janet Regnall
Telephone: (503) 284-5804
Rates: $30-$45

"The property was part of the original plot of land given to William and Elizabeth Irving in 1865," explains Janet, "and the area west as far as Grand Avenue is known as the Irvington area."

The English-Tudor style house, built in the 1920s, is located just below Alameda ridge on the east side of the Willamette River and opened its doors to guests last spring.

Treetop Room is a snug retreat with single bed, oriental rug, 1920s wicker chair, and plants, looking out into Douglas fir trees. The Garden Room, a large suite, is done in 1920s art nouveau style, with natural wicker settee and chairs, oriental rug, a potted palm, vintage oak washstand, and carved walnut bed.

A terrace overlooks the flower, herb, and vegetable garden on the east, and the backyard patio has a restful view of the grape arbor–both for guests' use. "I love cooking," says Janet, "so I indulge myself in preparing breakfast."

She uses fresh herbs from the garden in scrambled eggs, fixes a cheese plate, brews up Irish Breakfast or Earl Grey in a porcelain teapot, and grinds Italian roast beans for the coffeepot. Raspberries from the garden are pureéd and offered with a fresh fruit plate of banana half-moons and pineapple and cantaloupe chunks. Banana or blueberry muffins are ready to be popped out of the oven and drizzled with butter.

Janet, who has traveled far and wide, offers guests her extensive library of mysteries, novels, history, science fiction ("from my children"), film-making, travel, cooking, and women's literature. "It's an eclectic mixture, well-read and loved," she smiles.

For travelers who are in the Portland area for a few days, ask Janet about the information she's gathered on walking tours and country wine tours, of which there are a number in the tri-county area.

Golfers take note, for there are several public courses near Garden House. Try Rose City, which has 36 holes; or Broadmoor; or Colewood, which are out on Columbia Boulevard. I am partial to the front nine at Broadmoor–it must be what a Scotsman's palatial private estate would look like, with its rows of weeping willows and wide, long fairways.

For more information about what to see and do in the Portland metropolitan area, contact: Greater Portland Visitors Information Bureau, 26 S.W. Salmon Street, Portland, OR 97204. Telephone; (503) 222-2223.

COLUMBIA GORGE HOTEL

4000 Westcliff Drive
Hood River, OR 97031
Owner: Boyd Graves
Innkeeper: Glen Brydges
Telephone: (503) 386-5566
Rates: $78-$98

When in the early 1900s lumberman–philanthropist Simon Benson built a large hotel in Portland to promote travel to the Beaver state, he didn't stop there. His next project was to provide funds and impetus, as a member of the State Highway Commission, to construct the Columbia River Scenic Highway, making it possible for the first time to drive from eastern Oregon through the Cascade Mountains to the Pacific Ocean.

To make the trip more appealing to turn-of-the-century travelers, Benson built a tourist hotel in 1921 on a rocky bluff overlooking the Columbia River at Hood River. "Legend has it that Rudolph Valentino was a frequent guest," says innkeeper/manager Glen Brydges, "and Clara Bow, too." Apparently the red-roofed, Spanish-style Columbia Gorge Hotel became a favorite getaway for the rich and famous of the Jazz Age. "Notice the piano lounge just off the main lobby; it was named for Valentino."

The hotel, a rest home for many years, has been restored to its former elegance with an obliging staff, brass lamps, wingback chairs, Victorian wallpapers, and fresh flowers everywhere. One of the favorite guest rooms offers a king-size, antique, canopied bed and a cozy fireplace. The 46 guest rooms are spared a look-alike appearance by the use of lovely antique furniture, vintage mirrors and chests, rocking chairs, old-fashioned prints and chintzes, and fresh flowers.

As an overnight guest you will be served the hotel's sumptuous farm breakfast which includes a large assortment of fresh fruit; "honey from the sky," which the waitress drizzles onto your hot biscuits from dizzying heights; fresh-cooked oatmeal; followed by bacon, ham, sausage, eggs, and hashbrowns; and, finally, pancakes with warm maple syrup. If you still have room, try the cinnamon-baked apples–mouthwatering.

To help work off such a bountiful feast, try some of the easy trails around the nine acres of grounds, including a picture-snapping stop overlooking 125-foot Wah-Gwin-Gwin Falls, Columbia River, and gorge vistas. Notice the circular drive as you walk back to the wide front entrance . . . wasn't that Rudolph Valentino who just drove up in his burgundy Bentley?

To enjoy Simon Benson's highway project, the old Scenic Highway, drive east from Portland and Gresham via Stark or Burnside streets and follow the narrow asphalt ribbon as it winds through green Douglas fir and the gorge toward Multnomah Falls and Hood River.

INN OF THE WHITE SALMON

172 West Jewett Street
White Salmon, WA 98672
Owners/Innkeepers: Bill & Loretta Hopper
Telephone: (509) 493-2335
Rates: $55-$74

Located in the heart of the Columbia River Gorge, with its massive remnants of basalt from ancient volcanic flows, Inn of the White Salmon is on the Washington side of the river but is somewhat easier and quicker to reach from the Oregon side. White Salmon lies about 50 miles east of Portland on Interstate 80. If you prefer the slower route, take Highway 14 east from Vancouver through Camas and Washougal.

The inn was built in 1937 as the Hoodview Hotel, located in the shadow of Mount Hood and directly across the Columbia River from Hood River, Oregon. "We stayed at the hotel in 1972 and fell in love it it," recalls Loretta. "We bought the place in 1978 and began the restoration."

Each guest room has a personality of its own, decorated with Victorian wallpapers, antique brass or carved wood beds and four-posters, fluffy comforters, and thick towels. Extra touches, like antique hand mirrors, pin cushions, and perfume are laid out on vintage dressers and bedside tables.

Shaving mugs and brushes for the men and warm robes for hot tub users are provided. The tub is outdoors in the terraced garden. Beveled and gilt mirrors along with old pictures of roses and pastoral scenes adorn hallways and rooms.

Long before breakfast the smell of cinnamon and apples (and other savory scents) wafts down hallways into guest rooms. Round tables are laid with vintage china in rose patterns collected from hither and yon made to welcome guests to the inn's bountiful buffet.

How about Shrewsbury tarts, walnut poteca, Canadian butter tarts, lemon bars, Alsatian apple tarts or cinnamon toast flan? For seconds, try Georgia peach coffee cake, tart Mirabell (with prunes soaked in kirsch), hazelnut cake, date coils, or heavenly rolls. And for thirds (or fourths, or fifths) just a bite of cream cheese and raisin strudel, and the piece dé resistance, maple nut cream cheese sticky buns.

Your choice of egg dishes may include Hungarian pflauf (eggs, ham, and cheese enlivened with caraway seeds), chile rellenos, mushroom crust quiche, artichoke frittata, Polish sausage and eggs in cheese sauce, and mushroom and olive flan.

"I grew up in a Polish family in Ohio," explains Loretta. "Mother was a great cook, and we had many friends of different cultures and ethnic groups. I began collecting recipes from everyone; when we bought the inn and began serving breakfast, I wasn't satisfied with the commercial baked goods we were buying."

Out came the lifetime collection of recipes and cookbooks, and Loretta began baking. Every day. When the volume of business grew, "I could no longer bake everything myself," she recalls. "Now I have two local women alternate each day to prepare the pastries. They enjoy baking, and they have that loving touch I feel is important. I knew we had to do something unique and special to bring travelers here to White Salmon."

Bill Hopper, a former airline pilot, offers recreation trips, taking visitors on nearby wilderness dog-packing adventures or white water rafting on nearby rivers. "I might even show you where the best fishing holes are," he says with a wink. You'll see a selection of his adventure slides on a special screen in the breakfast room.

For additional information on what to see and do in the area, contact: White Salmon Visitors Information, P.O. Box 456, White Salmon, WA 98672. Telephone: (206) 493-3636.

A sampling . . . Eastern Oregon

FRENCH GLEN HOTEL

Frenchglen, OR 97736
Owner: Oregon State Parks Department
Innkeeper: Malena Konek
Telephone: (503) 493-2565
Rates: $39-$45

Travelers who are adventurous and seeking out-of-the-way places might like to sample the only inn located in the far southeast corner of the Beaver state, 60 miles south of Burns on Highway 205. With just eight postage stamp-sized guest rooms, it's almost too small to be called a hotel.

Constructed in the early 1900s, French Glen Hotel housed mostly sheepherders who grazed flocks in Harney County, once a Basque-rich area. Although the clientele has switched to travelers and vacationers, the simple building with its enclosed porch has remained the same except for the addition of indoor plumbing.

"The rooms are small, and we've used old-fashioned, small-scale furniture along with handmade quilts, many of which were made by my mother," says innkeeper Malena Konek, who leases the building from the Oregon State Parks Department.

The village has a population of about ten, depending on the time of year, and the number of buildings can be counted on one hand. Because it is located at the southern end of the enormous Malheur National Wildlife Refuge of more than 184,000 acres, the hotel draws birdwatchers, photographers, hunters, fisherpersons, desert lovers, and history buffs who seek out homesteads and ghost towns in the area.

There is a 42-mile self-guided auto tour winding through the refuge, the home and/or resting place for hundreds of thousands of geese, ducks, birds, and waterfowl following the Pacific Flyway migration route. Best times to see activity of animals and birds are at sunrise and sunset, especially in the spring and fall.

"When you come to French Glen Hotel bring an appetite," says a recent birdwatcher and photographer guest. Breakfast, like everything else in Harney County, is big. Try finishing two giant blueberry pancakes, two eggs, three sausages, and slices of watermelon, cantaloupe, and pineapple. "And plenty of fresh coffee to wash it down."

The evening meal (there are no other eateries at Frenchglen) is served family-style accompanied by lively exchanges of fishing exploits and tips, hunting adventures, and latest desert travel tips for ghost town buffs and wildflower lovers.

For more information about what to see and do in the area, contact: Harney County Visitors Information Center, 18 West D Street, Burns, OR 97720. Telephone: (503) 573-2636. And: Malheur National Wildlife Refuge, P.O. Box 113, Burns, OR 97720. Telephone: (503) 493-2323.

A late Victorian retreat . . .

Port Townsend

Beachcomb a driftwood-strewn beach, dig clams and find barnacle-encrusted oysters, climb a mountain, walk beneath arches of moss and 200-foot Douglas fir in a rain forest, explore an island . . . bed and breakfast travelers can roam far and wide on Washington's Olympic Peninsula, Whidbey Island, and nearby San Juan Islands.

Across Puget Sound from Seattle, on the peninsula, is Olympic National Park, where you'll find the only true rain forests in North America. Port Townsend lies north of the park along the Strait of Juan de Fuca, which divides the U.S. and Canada.

Most of the bed and breakfast inns in Port Townsend are lavish, high-ceilinged, restored Victorians dating back to Port Townsend's boom era of the late 1800s.

ARCADIA COUNTRY INN

1891 South Jacob Miller Road
Port Townsend, WA 98368
Owners/Innkeepers: Jim & Jennifer Shrout
Telephone: (206) 385-5245
Rates: $39-$63

"It doesn't look like a bordello anymore," says Jim. "In the 1920s and '30s the house was a speakeasy and, for a time, a house of ill repute. You can see where the old still was in back of the barn. Most of Port Townsend's hard liquor was made here during Prohibition days. The old-timers have great stories to tell about the place."

Jim and Jennifer Shrout spent about 10 years restoring the house. Arcadia Country Inn opened its winding driveway and farmhouse doors to bed and breakfast guests in 1984.

The eight guest rooms (all but one are on the second floor) are spacious and filled with antiques. The Master Bedroom has large corner windows, carpeting of soft beige, a queen size brass bed with dark blue floral comforter, and a rocking chair and window seat for relaxing. Its private

Victorian bath has a ceramic sink adorned with roses set into an old sideboard.

Other guest rooms have names like Garden Room, Maia's Room, Leif's Room, Jennie's Room, James's Room, and The Study–all with views of the garden, 70 acres of rolling meadows and trees, and the Olympic Mountains to the southwest.

In the entry, which is more like a large hotel lobby, are a large grand piano and a fireplace. In the adjoining dining room are round tables sporting red-and-white checkered cloths. One the oak bar the Shrouts set out a sustaining continental buffet–croissants and sweet rolls, fresh fruits, coffee, and teas. "Our guests also enjoy complimentary wine served at the oak bar," says Jennifer. "A far cry from being a roadhouse, then speakeasy, and waystop for Canadian booze smugglers," chuckles Jim.

HASTINGS HOUSE

313 Walker Street
Port Townsend, WA 98368
Owner/Innkeeper: Bruce Pierson
Telephone: (206) 385-3553
Rates: $50-$85

The Hastings House, constructed in 1891 by Frank W. Hastings, is one of those big old Victorians with the white-pillared porch extending across the front and around both sides. I expect to see ladies in white tea dresses and ruffly parasols there, sitting on wicker chairs enjoying a tete á tete and afternoon tea. The house was for some years the German Consulate.

An inviting entry hall is full of hand-rubbed oak woodwork and lovely fixtures. The guest rooms (some with shared bath) have names like Gable Room, Lace Room, Ivory Tower Room (with a view of the water and a turret sitting room), Rose Room, and Honeymoon Suite. All are pleasantly decorated in pastels, matching carpeting, and airy prints.

The most cheerful room on the main floor is the dining room-parlor with its potbellied stove, books and magazines, and windowsills filled with green plants. Guests are welcome to try the antique organ in the adjoining parlor. Breakfast, served at 8:30 a.m., includes "bread pudding, fresh baked cinnamon rolls, and fruit compote," says innkeeper Bruce Pierson. "We also invite guests to enjoy afternoon tea." Perhaps you should tuck in a tea dress and parasol, after all.

HERITAGE HOUSE

305 Pierce Street
Port Townsend, WA 98368
Owners/Innkeepers: Irene Ellis, Robert Ellis, and Patricia & James Broughton
Telephone: (206) 385-6800
Rates: $35-$75

"I never did like sand in my toes," confides Irene, "but I love to watch the ferries come and go. In Port Townsend you can be on the water if you want or up on a hill just seeing it all for miles and miles."

Heritage House is one of those extraordinary Victorians indigenous to this seacoast town–some say that Port Townsend has the best collection of restored Victorians north of San Francisco.

The Ellis and Broughton families brought to Heritage House an accumulation of some ten years of antique hunting, "in auctions, estate sales, and garage sales from the East Coast to Oregon," says resident innkeeper Irene. The flame mahogany four-poster in The Suite (two rooms with private bath) is circa 1790–1810 and was discovered near Portland, Oregon. "It's so high you have to climb in and slide out," laughs Irene.

The Blue Room has a hand-painted Victorian bed with matching dresser and wash stand. Suzie's Room, named after a granddaughter, is decorated a cheerful yellow and has a vintage iron bed. The Pink Room sports an antique galvanized tin tub–it folds up and rolls away, like the Saturday-night tubs of yesteryear.

History buffs will enjoy the formal Victorian parlor with its oriental rugs on natural wood floor, elegant settee and chairs, and traditional wallpaper.

Continental breakfast at Heritage House is served at the round oak table with its high-backed chairs in the formal dining room. "We serve fresh fruit compote with sweet rolls, coffee, and teas," says Irene.

James House
Port Townsend, Wa.

JAMES HOUSE

1238 Washington Street
Port Townsend, WA 98368
Owners/Innkeepers: Deborah & Rod LaMontagne
Telephone: (206) 385-1238
Rates: $40-$80

Staying at the James House, atop a hill overlooking the city and waterfront, it like visiting a wealthy aunt named Jessica or Emily.

Francis Wilcox James, a native of England, arrived in Port Townsend in 1853, two years after its founding. Some 36 years later, after such jobs as Indian agent, assistant lighthouse keeper, and store owner and customs inspector, the successful Mr. James and his wife Mary built the Queen Anne style house as their retirement home.

Mary died seven weeks after moving into the house, and Mr. James remarried in 1909. When he died in 1920, he left the largest estate accrued to that date in Jefferson County.

Guests at James House will appreciate the fine craftsmanship and materials in the house: parquet floors of oak, walnut, and cherry; newel posts, spindles, and bannisters of native wild cherry from Virginia still polished and beautiful; ornately carved brass door hardware; nine fireplaces, four of which remain in their original state with carved mantels and Minton tile.

"Some original furnishings remain–" explains Deborah. "Portieres on each side of the entry hall, the armoire in the Bridal Suite, and the two flowered chairs and matching settee in the library. Mr. James' beaver felt top hat, hat box, and his satchel, personal papers and books are displayed in the glass cabinet in the library."

Offering a selection of 12 guest rooms, James House is currently the largest bed and breakfast inn in Port Townsend. The Bridal Suite, with its own balcony and bay-windowed sitting room, was Mr. and Mrs. James' master bedroom. It offers a commanding view of Port Townsend Bay and the mountains beyond. "It's said that Mr. James was often seen sitting on the widow's walk off the suite, watching ships come and go in the bay," explain Deborah and Ron.

The guest rooms are decorated with period antiques, old china and porcelain, flowers and ferns, and many have a view of the water and mountains. Deborah serves a continental breakfast around the large oak table in the kitchen or in the formal dining room. "Guests like the old-fashioned wood stove and coziness of the kitchen," smiles Deborah.

LIZZIE'S

731 Pierce Street
Port Townsend, WA 98368
Owner/Innkeeper: Thelma Scudi
Telephone: (206) 385-4168; (206) 385-9826
Rates: $42-$79

Located 'uptown' in this seaport of some 6,000, Lizzie's is owned and operated by former antique dealer-construction contractor, Thelma Scudi, with part-time help from her teenage son and daughter. Thelma and I talked over a cup of coffee at the 12-foot country table that nearly fills the kitchen where the generous continental repast is eaten in the morning. "Lizzie Grant bought the house in 1887," explains Thelma. "It was really her house and she managed it herself. Captain Thomas Grant was a sea captain and was gone most of the time; he was an intermittently prosperous ship owner and seafarer."

Lizzie's photograph hangs in the music room–parlor. A grand piano, leather sofa, and chairs are grouped around the fireplace that is often lit in the evenings.

The house was built in the grand Italianate Victorian style, with characteristic 12-foot ceilings in all rooms on the main floor and ornate fireplaces–one in each parlor and one in Lizzie's Room, the master suite on the ground floor.

The other five antique-filled guest rooms are up the staircase on the second floor. "Most of these old Victorians started as homes of the wealthy in the late 1800s, early 1900s," says Thelma. "After a succession of owners, a measure of benign neglect, and often tenure as a apartment building or boarding house, 20th century entrepreneurs and ambitious couples are re-discovering their potential as bed and breakfast inns."

Occasionally, prospective innkeepers land on Thelma's ornate, carved doorstep, looking for ideas, advice. "If you have more style than sense, the stamina of an ox, and $500,000 in your pocket, give me a call," chuckles Thelma, who offers consulting services on bed and breakfast inns.

Thelma gets up for early morning coffee at the Bayview Coffee Shop, around sunrise (usually before guests awaken). "You need to take care of the important things . . . whether the ferry will be in on time, the color of the sunrise, and whether the grey whales are running . . . you have to take care of yourself in order to take care of others."

Lizzie's Kitchen

Other restored Victorian inns to sample on a bed and breakfast excursion through the Port Townsend area . . .

QUIMPER INN

1306 Franklin Street
Port Townsend, WA 98368
Owner/Innkeeper: Mariii
Telephone: (206) 385-1086
Rates: $44-$55

Built in 1880, Quimper Inn is a large square Georgian Victorian structure with a wide front porch supporting a roomy verandah on the second level. Innkeeper Mariii, an artist, has a penchant for creating stuffed objects, creatures, and dolls. Her creations are arranged in whimsical wall collages, on the beds, and tucked here and there on dressing tables, night stands, and even in an antique bed pan in six large, antique-filled guest rooms.

The common room on the main floor is a melange of stuffed objects, green plants, comfortable sitting places, polished wood floor, and large library of art books.

You'll be greeted by a stuffed chanticleer on the ample breakfast table where "a French petite dejeuner is served each morning," says Mariii. "Fresh ground coffee complements the baskets of boulangerie delights."

With names like Gaff Schooner, a two-room suite with antique tin tub, Laughing Whale, Blue Northern, with a garden view, Windjammer, and Brasspyglass, Quimper Inn is an experience in creative art, with its imaginative and dimensional gallery of objects d'art filling guest rooms, walls, and spilling onto floors–an entourage of unconventional and whimsical delights.

STARRETT HOUSE

744 Clay Street
Port Townsend, WA 98368
Owners/Innkeepers: Richard & Sue Thompson
Telephone: (206) 385-5619; (206) 385-2976
Rates: $50-$75

One of Port Townsend's largest structures, painted in shades of lavender, the Starrett House looked a bit faded and tarnished when I visited, but is a grand Victorian lady nonetheless. The Starrett House offers a gourmet restaurant, nine elegantly furnished guest rooms–the Bridal Suite, Master's Quarters, and the Morning Room have parlor stoves, and mountain and water views–a massive circular staircase and tower, and ceilings painted with allegorical figures. The Starrett House offers afternoon tea and tours in May during the annual Port Townsend Victorian house tour.

THE SUMMER HOUSE

2603 Center Road
Chimacum, WA 98325
Owners/Innkeepers: George & Maryann Nieminen
Telphone: (206) 732-4017
Rates: $35-$40

Built in 1912 by Charley Williams for his wife, Hanna, The Summer House was a small dairy on the Williams family 320-acre homestead. Milk was sold to the creamery at Chimacum. Minutes from Port Townsend, about 10 miles southeast on Highway 18, your room may overlook the duck pond or the nearby Olympic mountains.

Two comfortable guest rooms with shared bath on the second floor have antique brass beds. In the larger room is a cozy sitting area with wicker settee and chair. The smaller guest room is decorated in shades of rose and white.

"We have a duck pond, a wooden swing, and picnic table and chairs outside," says Maryann. "People like it because it's quiet and relaxing here."

Maryann serves a continental breakfast–often with her fresh-baked scones, cardamom bread (fresh from Seattle), or for special occasions, her baked Finnish pancake with strawberries and cream.

"Guests who like classical music might like to take in the Philadelphia String Quartet from Seattle," offers Maryann. "They have renovated an old barn about four miles from our place and will be giving weekend concerts."

LINCOLN INN BED & BREAKFAST

538 Lincoln Street
Port Townsend, WA 98368
Owners/Innkeepers: Joan & Robert Allen
Telephone: (206) 385-6677
Rates: $65

Joan and Robert Allen are transforming a unique brick Victorian into another of Port Townsend's old-world bed and breakfast inns. "The house was built by George Starrett for Elias DeVoe," says history-buff Robert Allen. "Elias owned a brick company and he had the two-story house faced with his own brick as a way of advertising his local product."

The Allens are renovating two large guest rooms upstairs. Carrie's Room was the original DeVoe master suite. It has the morning sun and a view of the bay. "We're using the original colors as much as possible," says Joan. "It's amazing what you find under several layers of linoleum and umpteen layers of paint. The wood floors are lovely and the original colors are soft pastels."

Robert also plans to open a restaurant in Port Townsend, down near the waterfront. Joan, from England and with twenty years experience as a flight attendant, will manage Lincoln Inn. "We want travelers to feel at home here," says Joan. "We'll serve wine in the parlor each evening and a sumptuous breakfast each morning. Bicycles will also be available to our guest for exploring the Port Townsend area."

The story of Port Townsend has all the elements of an epic novel–boom and bust growth (the railroad was built in Seattle instead), pioneer ruggedness, and gentility in the wilderness. A wild and woolly seaport in the past, Port Townsend's life is quieter now. Amid trees, water, and mountains (sometimes shrouded in fog and mist), artists and craftspersons have found refuge here. They paint, write, carve, print, record, stitch, compose, and sell what they make in restored Victorian waterfront shops.

The Wooden Boat Festival in September features hand-crafted boats and other maritime crafts such as canoe making, knotting, brass fitting, sail making, scrimshaw, and sea chanty singing.

For additional information about the Port Townsend area, write: Port Townsend Tourist Information Center, 2437 Sims Way, Port Townsend, WA 98368. Telephone: (206) 385-2722.

A Rural Island in the Sound . . .

Whidbey Island

Whidbey Island is a curious mixture of inlets, coves, bays, harbors, and passages . . . rolling farmland, stands of Douglas fir, and small vineyards . . . small villages, hamlets, and towns . . . folks who like island life and who say, "there are really two islands here, the north half and the south half." Reportedly the second longest island in the U.S. and the largest in Puget Sound, Whidbey Island is some 60 miles in length and just two to three miles wide in some places.

A naval air station on the north end booms with high-tech jets and hums with the activity of Oak Harbor, Whidbey's largest town. At center island, home of Coupeville, the county seat, ferries toot and blast their arrival at Keystone from Port Townsend and the Olympic Peninsula, a 30-minute ride. At south Whidbey, ferries disgorge cars and passengers at Clinton, a 15-minute ride from Mukilteo, north of Seattle on I-5.

Travelers will find at least eleven inns clustered at the center and the south end of Whidbey Island, with enthusiastic innkeepers offering bed and breakfast in charming old farmhouses, shingled custom-designed inns, glass and cedar mansions by the sea, rustic log cabins, and restored Victorians.

SALLY'S BED & BREAKFAST MANOR

215 Sixth Street
P.O. Box 459
Langley, WA 98260
Owner/Innkeeper: Sally DeFelice
Telephone: (206) 221-8709
Rates: $55-$65

Sally DeFelice spent eight months remodeling the small farmhouse perched on a gentle slope facing east toward Camano Island, Saratoga Passage, and mainland Washington. "I had vacationed on Whidbey Island here in the Langley area for many years," she said. "When I saw the old farmhouse for sale–and the view–I couldn't resist buying the three acres and moving to the island."

Two solar hot water heaters, one breakfast sun room and large outside deck, one rock fireplace, and two refurbished guest rooms with private baths later, Sally was ready for bed and breakfast travelers.

Her two guest rooms on the second floor offer a snug, country feeling with soft pastel prints, comfortable wingback chairs, baskets of apricot shampoo and special soaps, magazines, and views of the water. On the main floor are two common areas: a cozy living room with its rock-faced fireplace; and a dining room with cushioned window seat, Sally's well-stocked library, a stereo system, and shelf of travel information.

"One of the things I wanted was a large garden," recalls Sally. "Now I have plenty of room for vegetables and berries. Guests are welcome to work in the garden, pick strawberries, raspberries, and vegetables. My goal is to become as self-sufficient and conservation-efficient as possible. We churn our own butter, and we also have three compost bins next to the garden."

Raised beds are neatly arranged just a short walk across the lawn from the sun deck. "Later, we'll renovate the old barn and use it for small meetings, dinners, and receptions," she explains as we sit in the breakfast sun room eating muffins and a hot mushroom-bacon-egg dish, sipping juice and coffee. "The hot tub, on its own secluded deck, is also for guests' use. My goal is for people to come here and feel an atmosphere of peacefulness—a place to unwind and refill one's own cup."

WHIDBEY HOUSE

106 First Street
P.O. Box 156
Langley, WA 98260
Owner/Innkeeper: Priscilla Golas
Telephone: (206) 221-7115
Rates: $55

Located in downtown Langley near arts and crafts shops, eateries, and the local drugstore is Whidbey House. The long, narrow house that clings to a cliff overlooking Saratoga Passage has an inverted design, with the main floor at street level and three guest rooms tucked out of sight below. A long outside deck becomes the common area, an inviting place to pull up a chair for an afternoon of watching small boats, seals, whales, blue heron, and, occasionally, a bald eagle.

Priscilla Golas, flight attendant and innkeeper, furnished the guest rooms with antiques from nearby British Columbia along with matching linens, wallpapers, and curtains. Warm quilts and English chocolate truffles on bed pillows greet Whidbey House guests.

The continental breakfast of juice, fruit, and fresh rolls will be delivered to your room. "I plan to have a dining room on the main level of the house," says Priscilla. Until then, the spacious deck overlooking Camano Island, the passage, and Cascade mountains will do nicely.

THE ORCHARD BED & BREAKFAST

619 Third Street
Langley, WA 98260
Owner/Innkeeper: Martha Murphy
Telephone: (206) 221-7880
Rates: $32-$70

Close to downtown Langley and surrounded by an old orchard, Martha Murphy and her two children welcome travelers. Families with children are welcome to The Orchard Bed and Breakfast. "I love being an innkeeper," smiles Martha. "I enjoy spending time with guests in front of the old wood stove in the living room during the evenings."

Martha, who teaches children's theater, seems to have an abundance of energy for innkeeping as well. She cooks up a continental breakfast of juice, pastries, whole-grain breads, fresh fruit, and homemade jams and preserves.

There's a porch swing for sitting, a large yard for playing, lots of sitting places for reading or conversing, and the orchard for finding nuts and fruits. Two guest rooms on the second floor with shared bath provide comfortable havens of retreat. For rainy days there are lots of children's books and games. "I can recommend good babysitters for children of all ages," says Martha. The Orchard Bed and Breakfast is open seven days a week from June 15 through Labor Day and just on weekends the rest of the year. Weekly family rates are available.

SARATOGA INN BED & BREAKFAST

4850 South Coles Road
Langley, WA 98260
Owners/Innkeepers: Debbie & Ted Jones
Telephone: (206) 221-7526
Rates: $55-$65

Located on a hill with twenty-five acres of forest, meadows, and view, and within walking distance of downtown Langley, Cape Cod-style Saratoga Inn was custom built as a bed and breakfast inn in 1982 for former Californians Ted and Debbie Jones.

Five spacious guest rooms with private baths located on the second floor are named Queen Anne's Lace, Country Garden, Willow, Meadow, and Hollyhock. Each has individual homelike touches – an antique handmade quilt, a rocking chair, a white linen chaise, Franklin stoves in two rooms, a brass and iron bed, flowered or patterned bed linens, a nautical deck chair (reputed to be from the *Queen Mary*), a peeled pine headboard, and fresh flowers, English scented soaps, and bath powder.

Outside are sunny decks for lounging, brick walks and gardens for strolling. You might have afternoon tea in the treehouse, or borrow a bicycle, or play croquet.

One of the nice features at Saratoga Inn is the enormous common room on the main level. Dominated by a raised brick-hearth fireplace, the room contains a comfortable blend of country antiques, Chippendale, and Queen Anne sofas, chairs, and tables.

Guests leave full from the long dining room table after consuming an early morning continental breakfast of freshly ground coffee, croissants, bran or blueberry muffins, homemade blackberry jam, and seasonal fruits.

HOME BY THE SEA

2388 East Sunlight Beach Road
Clinton, WA 98236
Owner/Innkeeper: Sharon Fritts-Drew
Telephone: (206) 221-2964
Rates: $55

"I experienced two revolutions," says Sharon casually as we walk through the kitchen onto the outside deck with its hot tub and a full view of Sunlight Beach, Useless Bay, and Deer Lagoon.

"As in Central America?" I ask.

"No, earlier ones – Afghanistan and Iran," she answers.

I was impressed with her matter-of-fact and casual, yet warm and friendly personality. Sharon spent some time as an international teacher and has many stories to tell. Perhaps you can entice her to sit a spell in the living room, which overflows with hammered brass, intricately-carved rosewood, mysterious looking East Indian smoking devices as well as exotic fabrics, prints, and pillows. Images of a cacophonous street bazaar in New Delhi or Rangoon come to mind.

The large dining room table behind the rosewood screen where breakfast is served is equipped with field glasses for scanning the beach and Admiralty Inlet. "We set our clocks by the passage of the *Princess Marguerite* – she leaves Seattle at 8:00 a.m. – on her way to Victoria for the day," says Sharon.

Home by the Sea has two guest rooms with private baths on the second floor. Both rooms have grand views of Sunlight Beach and Useless Bay – home to hundreds of geese, ducks, gulls, sandpipers, heron, and a family of bald eagles. Reading nooks, treasures from around the world, and a potpourri of furniture combine comfortably. "We invite our guests to make a picnic lunch or fix a cup of coffee or tea in the kitchen – we want people to be comfortable here."

CLIFF HOUSE

5440 South Grigware Road
Freeland, WA 98249
Owner/Innkeeper: Peggy Moore
Telephone: (206) 321-1566
Rates: $100

Have you wondered what it might be like to live in a glass house? The floor-to-ceiling windows and massive beams create a spectacular effect at Cliff House, about 10 miles north of Langley. With a sunken living room and fireplace, a music alcove with its player piano, and the guest suite loft, where the moon and stars will be at your elbow, you may not want to depart.

"We find that couples who are celebrating a special anniversary or honeymoon like to stay here," says Peggy. "I prepare a continental breakfast and have everything arranged on the tables for guests to eat at their leisure in the morning."

There's a deck for watching ships (and perhaps a whale or two) go through Admiralty Inlet. There is a fireplace for warming body and soul, and primitive as well as contemporary art on walls and in secluded nooks. Notice the glass-enclosed atrium in the center of the house with its lush mosses, green plants, and ferns.

If you stay at Cliff House, you'll find a small box wrapped in pink foil on the bed–it will contain a sea treasure and a special poem. The last line says, "May your dreams be beautiful and your tomorrows hold joy."

PILLARS BY THE SEA

1367 East Bayview Avenue
Freeland, WA 98249
Owners/Innkeepers: Walker & Ellen Jordan
Telephone: (206) 221-7738
Rates: $50

Walker and Ellen Jordan have opened their turn-of-the-century, white-pillared home, situated at the south end of Holmes Harbor in the small community of Freeland, to bed and breakfast sojourners. "We came to Whidbey Island when Walker retired from the ministry in Michigan," says Ellen. "We enjoy the south end of the island, and we've met interesting people–often young businessmen will come here to retreat for the weekend."

With the entire second floor arranged for guests, including a private entrance, it is easy to find peace and quiet here. Two guest rooms, each with sitting areas, reading lamps, and private baths, are separated by a sitting room. Relax on the sofa with a reading lamp close by; white cottage curtains frame two windows behind you. Walk along the beach to nearby Freeland Park or explore tree-lined side roads out to Rocky Point, where Holmes Harbor and Saratoga Passage meet.

The day I visited Pillars by the Sea, Ellen was setting the antique dining table for breakfast with old china in a delicate rose pattern, cranberry crystal, and deep rose napkins tucked into mother-of-pearl rings laid on a hand-embroidered rose-dotted tablecloth. A vintage light fixture hung over the table.

Breakfast on old china coupled with a view of Holmes Harbor, directly out the patio windows, is one of those events that makes stopping at bed and breakfast inns memorable.

GUEST HOUSE BED & BREAKFAST

835 East Christenson Road
Greenbank, WA 98253
Owners/Innkeepers: Don & Mary Jane Creger
Telephone: (206) 678-3115
Rates: $35-$90

The large fresh-water pond, home for waterfowl, wildlife, and musical frogs, dominates the 25-acre landscape surrounding Guest House Bed and Breakfast. It's north of Langley and Freeland, toward the center of Whidbey Island. Don and Mary Jane offer a potpourri of accommodations, all with a view of the pond, resident deer, and a bald eagle or two.

The Farmhouse (vintage 1920s), and Sara's Room and Peggy's Room (with shared bath) offer antique-filled retreats. Guests have use of the living room with fireplace, TV, and family library and are invited to partake of Mary Jane's breakfast in the morning.

The Farm Guest Cottage, close by, has a large deck for outdoor lounging. Indoors, an antique parlor stove, private bath, and ample sitting-eating-sleeping area are decorated with antique treasures. Your continental breakfast of fresh croissants or sweet rolls is arranged on colorful print placemats on the round table.

Hansel and Gretel, a rustic log cabin with cement chinking, stained glass and criss-crossed paned windows is set amid Douglas fir up a path from the Farm Guest Cottage, close to the pond.

Climb seven rungs up the ladder to a log sleeping loft for a snooze, a relaxing spot with books, Indian rugs, weavings, and handmade quilts. It overlooks the living room, wood stove, and windows facing the wildlife pond. There is a fully-equipped kitchen.

The Carriage House used to be Don's workshop. It is nestled in the woods, yet is cheerful because of its stained-glass window in the arched entry, two skylights, and a picture window overlooking the wooded hillside.

"We used knotty pine on the walls and added the wood

stove, kitchenette, and bath," explains Don. Country antiques, flowers, wooden chests, and brown print linens and curtains create a warm, homelike retreat.

If the Guest House offers a 'piece de resistance,' it must be the Log Lodge on the edge of the pond. "We built it for our home," says Don. "When we moved down the path to The Farmhouse, Mary Jane left it decorated with our special collections and antiques because they seem to fit the log lodge dimensions and atmosphere."

The dimensions are regal. It's like having an enormous treasure-filled mountain lodge at your disposal for the weekend. There is a bear skin on the log living room wall and stuffed bear's head on the balcony railing watching from above.

Build an evening fire in the floor-to-ceiling stone fireplace in front of which is grouped a sofa, rocking chairs, rustic wood coffee table, fur pillows, green plants and flowers, native weavings, reading materials, and other antiques collected by Mary Jane and Don over the years.

The loft contains the master suite with its own parlor stove, cushioned and pillowed sitting area, desk, and bath.

Wrap up in a down comforter on the king-size bed and watch stars through wide glass windows at your elbow.

The Log Lodge also has a fully-equipped gourmet kitchen, sky-lighted dining alcove, and large outdoor deck for enjoying close-up views of the pond and resident waterfowl.

The Cregers provide a continental breakfast for each of the guest cabins and Log Lodge, including farm-fresh brown eggs, croissants or fresh-baked muffins, jams and jellies, hot or cold cereal with cream, fresh fruit or juice, and fresh coffee and teas (or hot chocolate if you prefer). "We find that people really unwind and relax here," says Don. "They just disappear for hours."

PENN COVE INN BED & BREAKFAST

Coveland & Alexander Streets
P.O. Box 628
Coupeville, WA 98239
Owners/Innkeepers: Dick & Joan Wieringa
Telephone: (206) 678-6868
Rates: $39-$45

"Oh, you're the one with the Oregon license plates," remarks Joan as she escorts me through her home in downtown Coupeville, about 28 miles from Mukilteo ferry at the south end, or three miles from Keystone ferry landing from Port Townsend.

I had been in town less than 30 minutes and was on my way to spend the night at The Victorian House, nearby, when I spotted the neat turn-of-the-century bungalow with its trim sign.

Joan and Dick offer three ground-floor guest rooms with pleasant 1920s decor. Each room has its own wash basin, and a full bath is shared. Breakfast is served in the sunny dining room. "We like the homey European concept of bed and breakfast," explains Joan. "We think it goes well with the quaint, old town atmosphere of Coupeville."

The Wieringas will offer ideas about what to see and do in the area, and you will have your own key to Penn Cove Inn, to come and go according to your own schedule.

THE VICTORIAN HOUSE

Sixth & North Main
P.O. Box 761
Coupeville, WA 98239
Owners/Innkeepers: Lee & Harriett Gray
Telephone: (206) 678-5305
Rates: $37-$48

"The first Coupeville Memorial Day parade we saw, in 1981, was the Boy Scout troop and one drum," recall innkeepers Lee and Harriett Gray with smiles. "This year we had everything, even floats and Queen of the Squash Festival, Mother Hubbard. Coupeville isn't behind the times–Coupeville time is whenever we get around to it."

"We bought the house [circa 1889] while Lee was still with the Lake Washington School District," explains Harriett. "He commuted for a year and a half while we renovated the property, which included Dr. White's dental office and an orchard behind the house." Dr. White's office is now Lee and Harriett's quarters.

Painted soft blue with white trim, The Victorian House was the two-story Italianate-style home of German immigrant farmer Jacob Jenne, his wife Bertha, and their three sons. Jacob later owned and operated the Central Hotel on Front Street; it burned many years ago, according to the Gray's research.

The house is restored, as authentically as possible, from the inside out. The Grays used many of their own family's pieces; notice the 'gout chair' in the parlor. Dating to the 1700s, it belonged to Harriett's family.

The clock in the high-celinged parlor ticks softly and chimes on the hour and half hour. Vintage sheet music sits expectantly on the old piano–"Beautiful Isle of Somewhere" and "Let the Rest of the World Go By." A four-legged swivel piano stool waits.

Lee comes in and lights the evening fire. Fellow guests share a bottle of Washington wine chilled by Harriett. The old parlor is filled with twilight conversation. We discuss families, children, education, Alaska, Navy life, flying, ferries, and restoring Victorian houses.

The fire dies down, embers wink softly. We say good-night and find our way upstairs to the two guest rooms with shared bath on the second floor that are filled with furniture and antiques from the family. There is a note to remind me to remove the old lace-fringed pillow shams. I climb beneath a handmade comforter; the old chestnut tree outside my window is a dark silhouette.

In the morning, Harriett rings the bell announcing breakfast and escorts us from parlor to dining room. We sit at the large old table drinking juice and admiring the fresh bouquet of purple iris as Harriett brings the first course–Lee's old-fashioned hot oatmeal with raisins, on which we pour gobs of cream and brown sugar–followed shortly by scrambled eggs and sausage, biscuits, and Harriett's homemade preserves.

Several cups of coffee later, along with amiable conversation, we go our separate ways. I visit Harriett's tiny old-fashioned gift shop just down the main hallway and buy a jar of her homemade marmalade to take back home.

For additional information about annual events and festivals, things to see and do, golf courses, historical museums, and such, contact: Langley Visitors Bureau, P.O. Box 403, Langley, WA 98260. Telephone: (206) 321-6765 (ask for 'Mo' Black). Central Whidbey Visitors Information, P.O. Box 152, Coupeville, WA 98239. Telephone: (206) 678-4066. North Whidbey Visitors Information, P.O. Box 883, Oak Harbor, WA 98277. Telephone: (206) 675-3535.

The Pearls of Puget Sound . . .

San Juan Islands

The San Juan Islands–those far-flung jewels in the northwestern corner of Washington State–lure bed and breakfast travelers onto wide ferry boats at Anacortes on Fidalgo Island, just north of Whidbey Island and some two hours north of Seattle. Like large turtles, Washington State Ferries (the *Elwha*, the *Kaleetan*, the *Evergreen State*) lumber steadily year-round from Anacortes to Shaw, to Lopez, to Orcas (the largest island), and on to Friday Harbor (the county seat) on San Juan Island. It takes about one hour to reach Orcas and another 30 minutes to reach Friday Harbor. There is also an international departure, at least once a day, from Anacortes to the islands and on to Sydney, British Columbia on Vancouver Island. Major islands in the San Juans are accessible only by ferry, boat, or plane (San Juan Airlines serves several, from Seattle). For ferry schedules/information contact: Washington State Ferries, (206) 464-6400.

THE CHANNEL HOUSE

2902 Oakes Avenue
Anacortes, WA 98221
Owners/Innkeepers: Sam & Kathy Salzinger
Telephone: (206) 293-9382
Rates: $38-$45

"We have to be flexible about breakfast because of the ferry schedules," says Kathy Salzinger. "The couple who likes to go to church on Lopez eat at 7 a.m., but most eat at 8 or 9." The eating sounds enticing–English tea muffins or scones (Kathy bakes every morning), with orange cream cheese (she whips it with grated orange rind, powdered sugar, and orange juice), juice, fruit, and fresh-brewed coffee.

"On weekends I do special ham, cheese, or mushroom souffles baked in individual ramekins. Try not to be late–they go flat quickly," she laughs. Breakfast is served on the daylight basement level in a fireplace room with French doors to the garden.

The Channel House is on Oakes Avenue, which takes travelers to the Anacortes ferry dock. The west guest room on the second floor has a great view of Guemes Channel and pastoral Guemes Island beyond. There is another guest room on the second floor with a sunrise view, and two guest rooms on the main level, behind the spacious living room–common area and library. There is a shared bath on each floor.

"Sam put in a hot tub for guests, and there are cover-ups and towels in each guest room," says Kathy. "A good place to watch sunsets and boats in the channel and unwind," adds Sam.

View from the Channel House

For more information about what to see and do in Anacortes (ask about the annual summer arts and crafts fair), the Skagit Valley, and nearby LaConner (restored Victorian village with unique shops) contact: Anacortes Visitors Information Center, 1319 Commercial Avenue, Anacortes, WA 98221. Telephone (206) 293-3832.

THE CHART HOUSE

P.O. Box 51
Deer Harbor, WA 98243 (Orcas Island)
Owners/Innkeepers: Don & Majean Palmer
Telephone: (206) 376-4231
Rates: $30 per person/per day

The Chart House deck, overlooking Deer Harbor with its boats coming and going from Pole Pass, is one of my favorite island places. "We gather here for breakfast at the picnic table on sunny mornings" says energetic Majean Palmer. "And again in the evening for a glass of wine, dinner, and the sunset," adds Don (he's a teacher, writer, and skipper of the Palmer's sailboat, *Amante*).

Two guest rooms on the lower level have their own patios and views of the harbor. Bali has a king-size bed, small refrigerator, sitting area, and private bath. Singapore, next door, offers twin beds, sitting space, and private bath. Both have picture windows and bright red Dutch doors. Visit Darwin, the rustic book-filled cottage just a few steps from the upper deck and above Don's garden.

"When the weather's right, we may take guests sailing with a picnic lunch," says the skipper. He's one of those safe skippers who's well-schooled in the craft–you might ask for some sailing lessons and try your hand at the tiller around Jones or Spieden Islands. Follow the sunset back in the twilight; it's usually one of those magenta and pink ones, fading to orange and navy blue (good for several frames of film and much ogling).

WOODSONG

P.O. Box 32
Orcas Island, WA 98280
Owners/Innkeepers: Carol & Alby Meyer
Telephone: (206) 376-2340
Rates: $40

A remodeled island schoolhouse (it was constructed in early 1900 and operated until the mid-1950s) has been transformed into a bed and breakfast retreat in a wooded area two miles from the Orcas ferry landing.

"It's a good place for bird watching," says Carol. "Particularly in the spring and fall when the water birds are migrating – visitors can see bald eagles, osprey, trumpeter swans, and blue heron."

Woodsong's guests stay in two large guest rooms with shared bath on the second floor and have the use of a large common room on the main floor. Ample sofa and cushioned chairs, wood stove, music system, well-stocked bookshelves, and an on-going chess game are welcome amenities.

Carol serves a continental breakfast during the summer season and a full repast during the winter season. "Crepes are one of my favorites to serve," says Carol.

A nearby riding stable offers trail rides and lessons, both English and western. There is also a golf course on the island. Orcas Island abounds with potters and artists; there are several potteries open to the public nearby.

KANGAROO HOUSE

North Beach Road
P.O. Box 334
Eastsound, WA 98245 (Orcas Island)
Owners/Innkeepers: Polly & Ken Nisbet
Telephone: (206) 376-2175
Rates: $25-$50

A five-guest-room bed and breakfast of the European tradition with shared baths down the hall, Kangaroo House is located about one mile north of Eastsound, Orcas Island's largest community. "It was the children who named Kangaroo House," explains Polly. "A sea captain, Harold "Cap" Ferris, brought home a kangaroo, named Josie, from one of his Australian voyages."

It seems that Josie loved music, rolled oats, and Mrs. Ferris' geraniums. According to old-time residents, neighbor children came often to visit Josie and named the house after her.

Common rooms are on the main floor and all the spacious antique-filled guest rooms are on the second. Breakfast is served at neatly set antique tables in the sunny dining room. There is a large deck for outside sunning and views of trees and meadows.

If time allows, drive around to Olga and visit the Orcas Island Artworks, where islanders display and sell handcrafted wares. If the Olga Store is open, plan a lunch stop—"excellent sandwiches," say local residents. A sunset stop atop 2,400-foot Mount Constitution (follow signs through Moran State Park) will net top-of-the-world views of Mount Baker, the lights of Bellingham, and many of the 175 San Juan Islands.

For more information about Orcas Island contact: Orcas Island Visitors Information Center, P.O. Box 252, Eastsound, WA 98245. Telephone: (206) 376-2273. Ask for copies of *The Island Sounder* and the *Orcas Island Map and Greeter.*

TUCKER HOUSE BED & BREAKFAST

260 B Street
Friday Harbor, WA 98250
Owners/Innkeepers: John & Evelyn Lackey
Telephone: (206) 378-2783
Rates: $40-$60

The turn-of-the-century Victorian that sits handsomely behind a neat picket fence has a new coat of grey paint and white trim and a small sign that says "Tucker House."

The innkeeper-couple has obviously put labor and love into the old house, including a red-tiled sun room off the kitchen where a continental breakfast is served. Children are welcome at Tucker House; there is a large, fenced play yard just beyond the sun room.

The two guest rooms and small detached cottage are clean, spacious, and have private entrances and private baths. The cottage has a comfortable sitting area with books, reading lamps, and music system, plus a small kitchen, private outside decks, and a sleeping loft.

Bustling Friday Harbor is a few blocks down the hill where there are lots of shops, eateries, the ferry landing, and marina–a kaleidoscope of color and activity.

San Juan Island abounds with history, and saving time for touring both ends of the island will be rewarding. Back in the 1840s both the English and Americans claimed sunny San Juan Island. One June day in 1859, so the records say, an American settler caught a British pig in his potato patch and shot it. By the end of that summer, American troops had 14 cannons trained on British warships in Garrison Bay.

Visit the two old posts, English Camp and American Camp, at opposite ends of the island and see photographs and artifacts telling the story of the 22-year stand-off. It's still called the Pig War, maybe because the pig was the only casualty.

Both camps are deserted now, save for the park rangers and a raccoon or two. The ranger at British Camp offers a 10-minute sound-slide presentation about the Pig War. Remnants of original buildings are guarded by giant maple trees at British Camp and by wild roses and Mount Baker at American Camp.

At the Whale Museum in Friday Harbor, you'll be chaperoned by whale talk (actual whale recordings) as you browse through the well-designed and informative exhibit. I left with a warm and wonderous feeling for the enormous mammals. If you sight any whales, particularly the striking black and white Orcas, the Whale Museum would appreciate a call on their hotline: 1-800-562-8832.

Other bed and breakfast accommodations in Friday Harbor include . . .

COLLINS HOUSE

225 A Street
Friday Harbor, WA 98250
Innkeeper: Leslie Stewart
Telephone: (206) 378-5834
Rates: $40-$45

A blue and white Victorian near the ferry landing, Collins House is conveniently located in downtown Friday Harbor. Innkeeper Leslie Stewart represents an absentee owner (leave a message at the Visitors Center if Leslie is away from the inn). Three guest rooms are neat and tidy and furnished with antiques. There's a small parlor for guests, spacious backyard and porches for sitting. Continental breakfast includes fresh-ground coffee and local fruit in season.

SAN JUAN HOTEL

50 Spring Street
P.O. Box 776
Friday Harbor, WA 98250
Owners: Norm & Joan Schwinge
Innkeepers: Randall & Fran Johnson
Telephone: (206) 378-2070
Rates: $40-$45

Dating back to 1873, the newly refurbished San Juan Hotel has 10 guest rooms furnished with antiques, old-fashioned print wallpaper, and crisp curtains. Continental breakfast is served in the parlor on the second floor, warmed by an antique, nickel-plated parlor stove on chilly mornings. Watch boats sailing and chugging in and out of the busy harbor while enjoying fresh-brewed coffee, muffins, juice, and a selection of teas.

For information about what to see and do on San Juan Island contact: San Juan Island Visitors Information Center, 450 Spring Street, P.O. Box 781, Friday Harbor, WA 98250. Telephone: (206) 378-5240.

View of Friday Harbor from San Juan Hotel

From the City to the Seashore . . .

Seattle and Beyond

Bordered by the massive Olympic mountains, Bainbridge Island, Vashon Island, and Puget Sound, Seattle has a large metropolitan area extending south toward Tacoma and Olympia and reaching north toward Edmonds, Snohomish, and Everett. Mt. Vernon, Anacortes, and Bellingham lie farther north, off Interstate 5.

Although seven rolling hills shape the Seattle skyline, it is the deep blue Sound, with its ships and waterfront hustle-bustle, that gives the city a romantic character. Seattle's roots run deepest in Elliott Bay, where the Sound meets the pier-lined waterfront.

CHAMBERED NAUTILUS BED & BREAKFAST INN

5005 22nd Avenue N.E.
Seattle, WA 98105
Owners/Innkeepers: Kate McDill & Deborah Sweet
Telephone: (206) 522-2536
Rates: $40-$60

Keri, resident Samoyed, barks hello from the white-pillared front porch as Kate opens the door into a wide, uncluttered entry hall. The Chambered Nautilus is a handsome, old, blue Georgian colonial built in 1915 for a professor at the University of Washington and perched on a wooded hillside close to the university.

All of the guest rooms are sizable and have that special appeal of light coming through old-fashioned paned windows. Common rooms on the main floor are enormous, filled with comfortable furniture grouped around a mantled fireplace. Just beyond is a sun porch which is being refurbished.

Afternoon tea and wine are served to guests, and the continental breakfast is prepared by Kate (she was formerly a baker in Seattle), including her fresh-baked rolls and breads as well as fruit, jams, and fresh-ground coffee. You can have breakfast in your room or join other guests in the dining room on the main floor where a parlor stove is fired up on chilly mornings.

The six antique-furnished, down-comfortered guest rooms, four with private sun porches, are on the second and third floors. Restful colors, rocking chairs, and an abundance of plants, books, and magazines create a homey atmosphere. "If you like jogging, you're welcome to join Keri and me for a morning run," offers Deborah.

If you like the friendly atmosphere of a university shopping area, there's one close by; a colorful melange of shops, tea rooms, boutiques, eateries and students.

GALER PLACE BED AND BREAKFAST

318 West Galer Street
Seattle, WA 98119
Owner/Innkeeper: Chris Chamberlain
Telephone: (206) 282-5339
Rates: $35-$45

Chris Chamberlain, new owner of Galer Place, came by her penchant for innkeeping naturally – she helped her aunt operate a 12-room bed and breakfast hotel in Littlehampton, England. "I plan to include some British traditions and decor at Galer Place," explains Chris. "For breakfast, I'll occasionally serve sausage rolls and Scotch eggs, along with fresh fruit with honey and yogurt and baked breakfast breads." She also plans to offer the traditional afternoon tea, "using my mother's 60-year old tea set."

On the second floor of the circa 1906 Victorian, located on Queen Anne Hill, are three guest rooms with shared bath called Oak, Brass, and Mahogany. The Oak Room has its own balcony overlooking the garden. The Brass Room has its own tiny stained glass window which reflects warm colors on the walls in the afternoon sun.

Guests may use the bay-windowed living room, filled with comfortable sitting places, plants, books, a music system, and TV.

Breakfast is served in the dining room, with its own lace-curtained bay window, at a polished wood table with old, leather-seated chairs. Guests also have use of the wooden hot tub outdoors in the enclosed garden.

"Because more and more women are traveling alone," says Chris, "I'm encouraging women travelers to try the bed and breakfast route. It's homey and safe and we often have lower off-season rates."

THE WILLIAMS HOUSE

1505 Fourth Avenue North
Seattle, WA 98109
Owners/Innkeepers: Susan & Doug Williams
Telephone: (206) 285-0810
Rates: $32-$49

Fringed with blooming azaleas, purple wisteria, and multi-colored roses, the large, square house, circa 1900, sits in a quiet, well-kept neighborhood atop Queen Anne hill, just above the Seattle Center and the monorail.

The formal oak entry hall is embellished with an unusual Italian hand-tiled fireplace, but it is the enormous old mahogany-framed, floor-to-ceiling mirror in the living room that catches my fancy. "It is one of the original pieces remaining in the house, in addition to the Italian fireplace," says Doug. "The home was well cared for by several owners and was once a boarding house for gentlemen."

There are five guest rooms with shared bath on the second floor. The English Room has morning sun; The Bay Room is the largest, with wide bay windows and original wallpaper; The Skyline Room has a view of the Space Needle and downtown skyline; The Brass & Satin Room is "vaguely scandalous," says Sharon; and The Emerald Room, quiet and secluded, overlooks trees and yard.

A roomy sun porch with wide, paned windows, a view of the city, wicker sitting places, and a plethora of green plants adjoins the living and dining rooms.

Guests assemble at the long, polished wood table in the dining room for Sharon's breakfast of hot fresh muffins or breads, eggs and cereals, fresh fruit and juices, and coffee and teas.

If you're interested in exploring, Queen Anne Hill lends itself to walking tours. Situated between Lake Union on the east and Elliott Bay to the west, the area was logged off and developed near the turn of the century, spawning many lovely neighborhoods. Around them are clustered a potpourri of parks, gardens, fashionable shops, and eateries.

If you've a penchant for old houses, ask for directions to Polson House (Queen Anne and Richardson Romanesque, circa 1905) on the east end of nearby Highland Drive; the Stimson-Griffith mansion (1904); Kerry mansion (1903); and the handsome Riddle House (1889).

For additional information about what to see and do in

Seattle, contact: Seattle-King County Visitors Bureau, 1815 Seventh Avenue, Seattle, WA 98101. Telephone: (206) 447-7273.

A 30-minute ride from Seattle on the Winslow ferry deposits bed and breakfast travelers on Bainbridge Island. Lying sheltered near the tip of the Kitsap Peninsula, Bainbridge is also accessible by Highway 104 from Port Townsend and by Highway 16 and Highway 3 from Tacoma.

You will find little information about Bainbridge Island in the usual guidebooks. It's small, rural, and full of salty bays and coves, providing space to get into the slow lane. Hidden away here are several bed and breakfast inns worth noting in your travel itinerary.

THE BEACH COTTAGE BED & BREAKFAST

5831 Ward Avenue N.E.
Bainbridge Island, WA 98110
Owners/Innkeepers: Eileen & Howard Werstiuk
Telephone: (206) 842-6081
Rates: $50 (two night minimum stay)

With a view of Eagle Harbor, The Beach Cottage is perched on barnacled pilings a few minutes from Winslow and the ferry dock. "We call it our Hansel & Gretel cottage," says Eileen.

It is 500 square feet of rest and relaxation. Sit on the porch and watch the activity in Eagle Harbor–sailboats, power boats, wheeling seagulls, and green-and-white ferries coming to and from Seattle. Or, build a fire and curl up by the fireplace on chilly mornings.

The Beach Cottage is filled with country furniture–a bentwood rocker, sofa, rattan coffee table, a round dining table. Eileen serves a substantial breakfast usually consisting of eggs, sausage, and hashbrowns with fresh-brewed coffee and teas. The Beach Cottage is not suitable for children or pets.

Bring along tennis rackets and try the courts at Eagle Harbor Waterfront Park, or spend an afternoon browsing through Winslow's many shops, eateries, and boutiques.

Lemon Tree Restaurant offers good sandwiches and is a place to see some of the local island folk.

THE BOMBAY HOUSE BED & BREAKFAST

8490 Beck Road
Bainbridge Island, WA 98110
Owners/Innkeepers: Georgene Hagen & Bob Scott
Telephone: (206) 842-3926
Rates: $39-$65

A large home–"we call it the captain's house," says Bob–built at the turn of the century, The Bombay House, with its pillared porches and its widow's walk, overlooks Rich Passage on the west side of the island. "We have a large garden filled with herbs and flowers," says Georgene. "Guests also enjoy the gazebo and watching boats in the Passage from our large outside deck."

Georgene and Bob offer one guest room on the main floor and three on the second floor. The largest room has a high, pine bed, comfortable sofa, parlor stove, and a view of the valley and Rich Passage.

Bed and breakfast guests gather around the dining room table for a continental breakfast of croissants, bran and cornmeal muffins, homemade jams and jellies, and papaya, melon, and bananas.

Close by there are canoes and sea-going kayaks for renting, a sandy beach, and a launching ramp. Or, rent bicycles and explore country island roads. Children ten and older are welcome at The Bombay House.

THE CAPTAIN'S HOUSE

234 Parfitt Way
Bainbridge Island, WA 98110
Owners/Innkeepers: Meg & Ed Hagemann
Telephone: (206) 842-3557
Rates: $30-$45

"Many of our guests carefully carry Heidi's pastries back home," smiles Meg. Heidi is an island baker who whips up mouth-watering European pastries. "She's baked since the age of four," explains Meg. "Her German grandfather taught her at their home in Buffalo, New York." Meg includes Heidi's special goodies in her breakfast, "and usually one of my omelettes–Ed says they're the greatest."

Although the guest rooms are small and share a bath, visitors will find them colorful and homey. The Harbor Room with its old-fashioned, paned, double windows is done in shades of rust, blue, and cream and looks out through the walnut tree to Eagle Harbor. The twin-bed room is done in blue and white gigham with "a Gloria Vanderbilt-designed comforter," says Meg.

Guests are encouraged to use the parlor, dining room, and living room at The Captain's House. Comfortable twin sofas flank the fireplace, the house library invites browsing, and watching the activity in Eagle Harbor from the porch swing is a favorite activity.

Meg and Ed can arrange a variety of sailing experiences for guests. Plan a gourmet picnic on the 26-foot *Stargazer* sailing to Blake Island; if Tillicum Village is a stop, try to see the Indian totems and displays of native arts, crafts, and carvings there. Or try a 4-hour dinner cruise on the 85-foot *Norden;* Poulsbo or the colorful Seattle waterfront are two possible destinations.

"If guests want to take the helm," says Ed, "the skippers will offer guidance and instruction."

Though it may take some effort, map-scanning, and plotting to get there, bed and breakfast travelers will be rewarded by discovering Bainbridge Island. For additional information about things to see and do contact: Bainbridge Island Visitors Information Center, 166 Winslow Way East, Bainbridge Island, WA 98110. Telephone: (206) 842-3700. For ferry information, Washington State Ferries: (206) 464-6400.

NO CABBAGES BED & BREAKFAST

7712 Goodman Drive N.W.
Gig Harbor, WA 98335
Owners/Innkeepers: Jamee Holder & Dal Winterowd
Telephone: (206) 858-7797
Rates: $30-$40

On the southeastern corner of Kitsap Peninsula, a few miles north of Tacoma, is another bed and breakfast inn for your travel itinerary.

"We love Gig Harbor arts and crafts," says Jamee. "I can see at least eight local handmade items in the living room--clay, weavings, an abstract oil painting. I call it eclectic ambience and Dal refers to our place as 'vintage hippie'."

There's also a handsome display of fishing flies on one wall by Oregon coast artist, Tony Hill. "It's a fun conversation piece. Dal likes to talk to guests about fishing," says Jamee, "and he'll take them out in our aluminum boat to see the harbor if they're interested."

No Cabbages sits on a bank overlooking Gig Harbor and the small town. "It's really a working Yugoslavian fishing village," explains Dal. "The fishing fleet just left for Alaska and our guests watched the goodbye ceremony. All the boats honk their horns as they cast off and leave the harbor while lights blink on and off in homes all around the harbor. It's a very special goodbye until September."

Bed and breakfast visitors find two snug, knotty-pine paneled guest rooms with warm, rust wool carpeting and cream-colored canopies over beds built up high, "so you can see the harbor when you wake up in the morning."

For breakfast, Greek or Mexican omelettes, popovers, fruit salad, and flavored coffee (amaretto or cinnamon may be on hand) are served at the harbor-view end of the large living-dining room.

"I love to read," says Jamee, "and guests are welcome to browse through our library–it's eclectic, too. A guest from northern California was reading a book by Robertson Davies; I let her take it home to finish and then she'll mail it back." No Cabbages is for relaxed, unstructured folks.

Most of the collection of imaginative shops and eateries in Gig Harbor, of which there are 35-40 down by the bay, are owned and operated by women: Beach Basket, White Whale Gallery, Mostly Books, The Bath Locker, and Scandia Gaard, a 105-year-old home, later a barn, now occupied by a Scandanavian giftshop and restaurant on Peacock Hill Road.

For further information about the Gig Harbor area, contact: Gig Harbor Visitors Information Center, P.O. Box 1245, Gig Harbor, WA 98335. Telephone: (206) 851-6865. And: Tacoma-Pierce County Visitor Bureau, 735 St. Helens, Tacoma, WA 98401. Telephone: (206) 627-2175.

UNICORN'S REST BED & BREAKFAST

316 East 10th Street
Olympia, WA 98501
Owners/Innkeepers: Rita & Hal Keating
Telephone: (206) 754-9613
Rates: $39-$43

Located just six blocks from the Washington state capitol grounds and downtown Olympia, Unicorn's Rest Bed and Breakfast opened its doors last May and is one of the first bed and breakfast inns in the Olympia area.

Two guest rooms, both on the second floor (shared bath), have dormer windows and plenty of space. Nimbi's Corner Room has country colors of blue and yellow, an antique armoire, and rag rugs. Aerie Room has an antique bed, French wallpaper, and a bentwood rocker for sitting. "In a book we have about unicorns," says Rita, "Nimbi is one of the most elusive of the unicorns. In his wanderings he returns to favored spots where he can rest. We thought it would add a touch of charm to name one of the rooms Nimbi's Corner–and perhaps generate some conversation."

The house, 1937 Cape Cod-style salt box, is painted white, "with blue trim and a blue door," explains Rita. "We bought the house and renovated it for bed and breakfast." The Keatings' two college-age daughters as well as a friend assist with innkeeping chores.

Guests at Unicorn's Rest have the use of a comfortable living room, the dining room, and kitchen (on request). Rita and her daughters serve an "expanded continental breakfast of juices, fresh fruit plate, a special quiche, and croissants, along with bacon or sausage."

"We hope our bed and breakfast guests will return to favored places as did Nimbi," smiles Rita.

For information about things to see and do in the Olympia area, contact: Olympic Visitors Information Bureau, 525 Washington Street, Olympia, WA 98501. Telephone: (206) 357-3370.

Into the Washington Cascades . . .

Washington Interior

Five major highways cross the Cascade Mountains into central and eastern Washington–Highway 20 through the North Cascades (western section closed during winter); Highway 2 over Stevens Pass; Interstate 90 over Snoqualmie Pass, Highway 12 over White Pass, and Highway 14 along the Columbia River.

Travelers head across Stevens Pass from Everett, winding through farm country to Startup, where the mountains begin in earnest. Wind up along the Skykomish River through tiny Skykomish, an old logging town, and through the Snoqualmie National Forest.

Mount Index dominates the skyline, and you will see the west portal of the lengthy Great Northern (now Burlington) Railroad tunnel as the highway climbs toward 4,061-foot Stevens Pass. Before descending to Icicle Valley and Leavenworth, bed and breakfast travelers will descend Tumwater Mountain through Tumwater Canyon.

BROWN'S FARM BED & BREAKFAST

11150 Highway 209
Leavenworth, WA 98826
Owners/Innkeepers: Wendi & Steve Brown
Emily, Jennifer & Peter Brown
Telephone: (509) 548-7863
Rates: $40-$45

"Steve wanted a log house and I wanted a Victorian," recalls Wendi. "We compromised and built what I call a country farmhouse." The family project began in 1978, and even the children helped peel bark from lodgepole pine and fir logs used as beams.

The design of the cedar and log home includes three gables, multi-paned windows, handmade cedar doors, and stained-glass accents made by Steve. Rocks were gathered from Icicle Valley for the huge stone fireplace that fills one wall of the family room.

Around the corner a kitchen with open cupboards and wood cook stove provide an informal, rustic place to whip up a hearty breakfast for guests. Cooked jointly by Wendi and Steve, breakfast might include fresh berries from the garden, omelettes with eggs from residents chickens, French toast, fresh blackcap jelly–the berries grow wild nearby–and homemade bread or muffins. "And my homemade salsa," says Wendi (she cans fruits and vegetables which can be seen in the large pantry).

Curl up under a homemade quilt in one of the two guest rooms on the main floor, and munch Aplets and Cotlets, sweets made in nearby Cashmere, compliments of the Browns. Read by the fire, hike into the woods or explore nearby Chumstick Valley, get acquainted with the family horse Misty, or lend a hand gathering eggs. In the winter, nearby roads provide cross-country skiing or snowshoeing areas.

Children are welcome at Brown's Farm. "Jennifer and Emily help clean the guest rooms," explains Wendi. "They're learning early that it takes work to be an innkeeper, but they enjoy our guests, especially if there are children along."

Brown's Farm Bed and Breakfast is an experience in informal, rustic farm living. "Don't bother to bring an alarm clock," says Steve. "The roosters do their thing every morning."

EDEL HAUS BED & BREAKFAST

320 Ninth Street
Leavenworth, WA 98826
Owners/Innkeepers: Mark & Betsy Montgomery
Telephone: (509) 548-4412
Rates: $30-$50

It looks like an elegant, well-manicured and freshly-painted Swiss or German hostelry. For some three years, since they opened in 1982, Mark and Betsy Montgomery have welcomed guests to Edel Haus Bed and Breakfast in downtown Leavenworth.

Memories of pensions in France and Belgium with French doors opening wide to the mountains are reflected in antique-filled, provincially-decorated guest rooms with flower-boxed windows looking toward the Cascades.

The two-course Edel Haus breakfast is gourmet–fresh fruit, sweet breakfast breads, perhaps French toast with cinnamon, homemade applesauce, baked eggs in cream, German sausage, plus fine ground coffee and teas.

Sun on the deck or patio overlooking the park; don swim suits, climb three steps and sink into the resident hot tub; walk down to Leavenworth's shop-filled main street and find everything from fine Swedish crystal to antique German Christmas ornaments.

"Thousands of people come each December for our Christmas Lighting Festival," says Mark. "It's becoming as popular as our Autumn Leaf Festival in September and October and the Mai Fest in May. The season in Leavenworth is all year around now."

HAUS ROHRBACH PENSION

12882 Ranger Road
Leavenworth, WA 98826
Owners/Innkeepers: Bob & Kathryn Harrild
Telephone: (509) 548-7024
Rates: $42-$65

"About twenty years ago Leavenworth was a dying community," explains Bob Harrild, "Project L.I.F.E. (Leavenworth Improvement for Everyone) was initiated by concerned townspeople, and the community adopted a new image, a Bavarian village."

Highlighted by Swiss and German-style gingerbread decor and bright colors, the Bavarian theme is carried throughout the shops, galleries, eateries, and hostelries of Leavenworth, including Haus Rohrbach Pension, located on 15 acres overlooking it all. "We host about 800,000 visitors every year in Leavenworth," say the Harrilds.

From humble beginnings in the 1920s as a railroad construction camp for engineer John Stevens and his Great Northern Railroad construction crew, Leavenworth has become a well-known tourist mecca. "All kinds of people have discovered Leavenworth," says Bob. "We have artists, photographers, writers, fisherpersons, river rafters, skiers, as well as sightseers–but not many railroad workers or lumbermen anymore."

Staying at Haus Rohrbach is like living in a Bavarian lodge. Children are welcome to the large home which was built in 1975 by William L. Rohrbach for his family of fourteen. "They had stayed in similar lodgings in Switzerland," explain Bob and Kathryn.

Many of the guest rooms and the common room below open to wide balconies overflowing with flower boxes and offer views of mountains, meadows, farms, and livestock. Functional guest rooms have hand-crafted wood beds and chests, fir wainscoting, white walls, and patterned curtains and spreads. Baths, which are shared, are down the hall.

Breakfast, served at 8:30 each morning, may include Kathryn's cinnamon rolls or homemade breads, omelettes, and plenty of fresh coffee and teas. In the adjoining common area, comfortable sofa and chairs and warm wood stove beckon guests tired from sight-seeing, hiking, or cross-country skiing, from fishing in nearby Lake Wenatchee, or from rafting in nearby white-water rivers. "Folks enjoy our new swimming pool and hot tub, a modern touch we added last year," says Bob.

For further information about Leavenworth festivals and things to see and do in the area, contact: Leavenworth Visitors Center, P.O. Box 313, 226 Eighth Street, Leavenworth, WA 98826. Telephone: (509) 548-7914.

EM'S BED & BREAKFAST

304 Wapato Street
Chelan, WA 98816
Owner/Innkeeper: Marlene Schlittler
Telephone: (509) 682-4149
Rates: $25-$40

Located on Highway 97 some 35 miles north of Wenatchee, often called the Apple Capital of the world, Em's Bed and Breakfast welcomes travelers to the Lake Chelan area. Constructed in 1890, the home has double-brick and plastered walls and "was quite contemporary for its time," says Marlene. An old-fashioned lamp post with five round globes greets the traveler by the front walk.

Four guest rooms with shared baths wait on the second floor. One of the larger rooms has a fireplace, blue and white pin-striped comforter, dark blue rug, tie-back curtains, and red accents. Other rooms are done in greens, yellows, and greys.

Marlene serves a full breakfast–often an egg casserole, special quiche, and hot breakfast rolls or fresh biscuits.

Em's is close to downtown Chelan, which has unique shops and a restaurant, the historic Campbell House, dating back to 1901, when it was a stage stop. In days gone by, before the dams were built, "paddlewheelers steamed upriver to Chelan and back down the Columbia River to Portland," says Marlene.

"Many vistors like to take the 55-mile boat trip up Lake Chelan, a fresh-water fiord reaching into the North Cascades," says Marlene. "It's a spectacular all-day trip on *Lady of the Lake II.* She accommodates about 350 passengers and leaves Chelan at 8:30 each morning during the season."

An old campers' and hikers' village, Stehekin was a base for forays into the Cascade Mountains at the turn of the century, long before the development of North Cascades National Park. Pack trips into the wilderness are available. Daily cruises and plane trips begin around May 15. Ask if the dinner cruises on *Lady of the Lake I* are still being offered; "we call her the 'old lady,'" smiles Marlene.

For additional information, contact: Chelan Visitors Information Center, Box 216, Chelan, WA 98816. Telephone: (509) 682-2022. Lake Chelan Boat Company, Box 186, Chelan, WA 98816. Telephone: (509) 682-2224. North Cascades Park, 800 State Street, Sedro Woolley, WA 98284. Telephone: (206) 855-1331.

LAKE PATEROS BED & BREAKFAST

206 West Warren Street
P.O. Box 595
Pateros, WA 98846
Owners/Innkeepers: Bob & Charlene Knoop
Travis and Courtney Knoop
Telephone: (509) 923-2626
Rates: $35-$40

"The house was built in 1922 for a retired naval officer and his wife," explains Charlene Knoop. "We like the country feeling of the place–the French doors and sunny windows, especially the sun room."

The two guest rooms have antique bed frames (one, tall oak and the other, a walnut four-poster), down pillows, and homemade quilts. The rooms share a bath-and-a-half. Downstairs on the main level, the spacious living room, dining room, and sun room have spring-green carpeting with navy and white accents (notice the old sewing machine and Charlene's collection of antique plates in the dining room).

Charlene and Bob serve a waist-bulging breakfast worthy of American bed and breakfast tradition. First, fresh fruit, coffee or tea and fruit juice, followed by a giant, puffed oven pancake or country omelette, made with farm-fresh eggs, hash browns, cheese, olives, mushrooms, almonds, and sour cream.

Guests may use the kitchen, laundry facilities, and outdoor barbeque on request. A second refrigerator on the patio can be used as well.

Located 19 miles north of Chelan on Highway 97, Pateros is in the Methow Valley, where the Methow River joins the Columbia. "The portion of river between Wells Dam and Chief Joseph Dam is Lake Pateros," explains Bob. "It's a year-round water recreation, hiking, and ski area; we get lots of sunshine and less than 15 inches of rain."

If you're in the area in the fall, try fresh-harvested Wenatchee and Methow Valley apples. Choose from Delicious, Winesap, Jonathan, and Rome Beauties. "The apple harvest continues into early November, unless we have an early freeze," says Charlene.

You'll recognize Lake Pateros Bed and Breakfast by sighting the colorful Japanese flying fish which often waves atop the Knoop's flagpole.

For more information about events and recreation, contact: Pateros Visitors Information Center, General Delivery, Pateros, WA 98846. Telephone (509) 923-2231.

DAMMANN'S BED & BREAKFAST

716 Highway 20 South
P.O. Box 26
Winthrop, WA 98862
Owners/Innkeepers: Hank & Jean Dammann
Telephone: (509) 996-2484
Rates: $25-$35

"As a rule, we have a dry climate with lots of sunshine and lots of snow in the winter, usually with a week or so of 25 to 35 degrees below zero," says Jean.

You may think you've reached the end of the road or the last outpost (it was, back in the late 1800s) when you arrive in the North Cascades old-west town of Winthrop. The western section of Highway 20 to Winthrop closes during winter; the eastern section is kept open. You are, in fact, surrounded by the Okanogan National Forest; Pasayten, a Cascade mountain wilderness; and a game refuge.

"You won't find many neon lights or much big-city life here," says Hank. "But if you're looking for a horse to ride, a wilderness to explore, a mountain trail to hike, or a river to fish, just sit a spell and we may work something out."

Hank and Jean offer two pleasant, antique-filled guest rooms with patchwork quilts, one of them overlooking bubbling Methow River. The downstairs guest room opens onto a small patio. Guests may use both the patio and deck overlooking the river, or move close to the fire in the living room with a good book.

You'll want to explore downtown Winthrop with its rows of western false-fronted buildings, wooden sidewalks, and 1890-style street lights. Stop by the Mountain Gallery featuring western and wildlife art by a dozen or so local artists.

Even the annual events have a western flavor: Dog Sled Races and Snowshoe Baseball Tournament in January; Mule Days Rodeo and Antique Auto Rally in September; and 49'er Days and River Rat Days in May and July.

"Lots of folks come back," say the Dammanns.

For further information, contact: Winthrop Visitors Information, P.O. Box 402, Winthrop, WA 98862. Telephone: (509) 996-2125. Cascade Loop Association, P.O. Box 225, Chelan, WA 98816. Telephone: (509) 682-5667. For Highway Pass Report: (509) 663-5151.

North of Seattle . . .

The North Coast

Snohomish is one of those western Washington names of native Indian ancestry that rolls off the tongue like Tulalip (an Indian reservation north of Everett); Mukilteo (where a ferry runs to Whidbey Island); Skykomish (a small hamlet towards Stevens Pass and Leavenworth); and Lummi (an island near Bellingham).

Located about 30 miles north of Seattle and seven miles east of Everett, Snohomish is an old-line dairy town dating back to 1860, when 27-year-old E.C. Ferguson framed up a house in Steilacoom (south of Seattle) and barged it by boat upriver to be assembled at the site of what is now Snohomish. The town is now on the State and National Historic Register.

COUNTRYMAN'S BED & BREAKFAST

119 Cedar Street
Snohomish, WA 98290
Onwers/Innkeepers: Sandy & Larry Countryman
Telephone: (206) 568-9622
Rates: $40-$50

"My mother cried when we bought the house," recalls Sandy Countryman. "But we rolled up our sleeves and began the cleaning, scraping, painting, and wallpapering."

The 'tract house' Victorian (Sandy says the house plans cost one dollar in those days) was built in 1896 as a doctor's office and residence. "It has four floors and twenty-eight rooms," explains Sandy. "It's a wonderful old house and we do welcome families with children here."

Bed and breakfast travelers will find four guest rooms (shared baths down the hall)–two on the main level and two on the second floor. The fireplace room (second floor) has a brass and iron bed with a quilt made by Sandy and her mother, along with pillow shams from the Victorian era. Antique lamps sit on bedside tables, a pair of wicker chairs and matching table sit comfortably by old-fashioned ruffle-curtained windows.

Leaded glass French doors open to the inside balcony which overlooks the main entry hall, one story below. In the room is a display of 1919 fashion art. "The exhibits change," explains Sandy. "We have an art gallery and framing service on the main floor."

Guests at Countryman's Bed and Breakfast get to choose what they want for breakfast. "One morning we had rainbow trout," says Larry. Sandy's blueberry muffins, hot from the oven, are favorites. The oak table, eight feet long, accommodates lively morning discussions.

Other common areas open to guests are the living room and library/den. "For a house that was once mortgaged to Montgomery Ward for the bathroom fixtures, Mother agrees that it's looking pretty good again," says Sandy.

Ask Sandy and Larry about their 45-minute guided tour of historic Snohomish. Perhaps there will be additional folklore and facts about the intrepid E.C. Ferguson and others who settled this rich dairyland area.

CHUCKANUT BED & BREAKFAST

312 Blanchard Road
Bow, WA 98232
Owners/Innkeepers: Carol & Don Shank
Telephone: (206) 766-6940; (206) 776-6667
Rates: $30

When I asked Carol for directions to Bow, she laughed and said, "Well it's about two-and-a-half miles north of Edison on Chuckanut Drive." Which means, head north from Seattle about 60 miles (on I-5 toward the Canadian border) and take a side trip on Highway 11 from Burlington. Bow is located in Skagit County, just south of Bellingham and north of Anacortes.

On a hill with a grand view of Samish Bay, Samish Island, and the San Juan Islands (including Lummi Island to the north), Chuckanut Bed and Breakfast is a place to retreat and restore body and soul. No one will bother you here, no telephones will ring, no salesmen will call.

Walk eleven steps down to your own private entrance into a small suite warmed by pale yellow wallpaper, wall-to-wall carpeting, and view. There's a small kitchenette and private bath. Trek upstairs and sit on the large deck overlooking 180-degrees of salt water, green island gems, sailboats, and seagulls.

"The atmosphere here is very comfortable and rustic," says Carol. "If you're looking for an elegant ocean resort with wall-to-wall room service, you'll be more comfortable in another location."

For those who like to hike, there are several easy day treks. If you bring your bicycles along (as many Northwest travelers do), there is good biking on the flat area just before the road climbs higher on Chuckanut Drive.

Guests have a choice – breakfast makings in the suite or "a large continental breakfast at our new restaurant, the Rhododendron Cafe, just down the road." You'll have fresh baked breakfast breads; sunshine, blueberry, or walnut muffins; as well as fresh fruit and plenty of coffee, juice, and teas.

"Within-two-and-a-half miles are what we think are four great restaurants," says Carol. "Oyster Creek Inn, Oyster Bar, Chuckanut Manor (dancing on weekends), and our place."

The Shanks have their own herb garden (thyme, oregano, chicory, mint, marjoram, rosemary) and use fresh herbs in their cooking. They make their own pasta, cook fresh seafood, fresh poultry, and have a nightly stew – perhaps a Spanish paella, chicken with spinach dumplings, or couscous (a Moroccan peasant stew with lamb and vegetables over crushed grain).

"We've had people from as close as ten miles away stay with us," says Carol, "and from as far away as Switzerland."

WARNER HOUSE BED & BREAKFAST

611 North Garden Street
Bellingham, WA 98225
Owner/Innkeeper: Jean Warner
Telephone: (206) 671-0995; (206) 676-9884
Rates: $30-$40

Located in Washington's northernmost county, Whatcom, and just across the campus from Western Washington State University (see the outdoor sculpture exhibit there), Warner House offers two pleasant guest rooms (shared bath). "One of them has a grand view of Bellingham Bay and the city," says Jean.

Warner House is convenient to Western for visiting professors and families (Jean welcomes children but prefers no pets). Breakfast is a full one and may vary from special egg dishes to chipped beef on toast.

For an uncommon shopping experience, try Fairhaven Village (11th Street near Harris) at the head of Chuckanut Drive. Old, brick buildings dating back to the late 1800s house a collection of shops offering cookware, books, ice cream, Mexican apparel, fine wines, and 23 other kinds of goods (plus several good eateries).

If you like wide-angle views, try Chuckanut Drive (Chuckanut is a word the Indians reportedly used for anything important to them). Hugging the cliff overlooking Bellingham and Samish Bays, it was the first scenic road built in Washington. "Whenever we want visitors to leave the area with a good impression," says Jean, "we take them up on Chuckanut Drive."

WEST SHORE FARM BED & BREAKFAST

2781 West Shore Drive
Lummi Island, WA 98262
Owners/Innkeepers: Carl & Polly Hanson
Telephone: (206) 758-2600
Rates: $25-$40

"One day I came home from running errands and found a salmon wrapped in newspaper in my refrigerator," says Polly Hanson. "Or it may be cod or halibut–the fishermen on Lummi are like that; they pay Carl in fresh fish when he does welding for them."

Carl (he was a Boeing engineer) and Polly (she was a library director in King County) moved to Lummi Island from the Seattle area in 1975. They built their octagonal house with native woods (red cedar, Alaskan yellow cedar, maple) and large windows to take advantage of the sweeping marine view at their doorstep. "Our friends say it's rustic modern," add the Hansons.

Set into the side of a hill and with solar greenhouses on two sides of the octagon, the house is heated with wood (the Fisher stove is in the basement). "I have a wood cookstove next to the Jenn-Air in the kitchen, which is nice on chilly mornings," says Polly.

Breakfast at West Shore Farm Bed and Breakfast is a

solid one–perhaps a fritatta with eggs, mushrooms, vegetables, cheese; ham or bacon; croissants or muffins; waffles with fresh strawberries or raspberries; homemade syrup; and Polly's crabapple jelly. "And fresh milk, cream, and butter from our Jersey cow."

There are country comforts in the guest rooms (shared bath)–wall-to-wall carpeting, electric blankets and comforters, sitting places. "I think the world must be full of tired people," smiles Polly. "Guests say they are going to get up early but they never do."

Relax on the deck and watch the tide come and go; spot Orcas and Clark and Matia Islands to the west; walk on the beach and collect driftwood treasures; identify and watch marine birds; enjoy the Hanson's library (stocked with humor, short stories, island history, old books). "Guests also enjoy our sauna which we built of cedar and rocks from the beach."

For a nominal cost, the Hansons offer lunch and dinner options, "because we have only one restaurant on the island and it operates on its own time schedule–we always say that it's a pleasant surprise if it's open."

To reach Lummi Island, drive north from Bellingham, taking exit 260 onto Slater Road, then Haxton Way to ferry landing (about 10 miles). The Hansons can also arrange transportation (for a small fee) from the Bellingham airport.

For information about what to see and do in the Olympia area, contact: Olympia Visitors Information Bureau, 525 Washington Street, Olympia, WA 98501. Telephone: (206) 357-3370.

British Columbia . . .

In and Around Vancouver

It is a straight 135-mile drive on Interstate 5 north from Seattle to downtown Vancouver, British Columbia's largest city. The setting is spectacular. Visit Stanley Park, walk the Capilano suspension bridge, ride the Grouse Mountain skylift, take in the largest Chinatown north of San Francisco and Vancouver's answer to Seattle's Pike Place Market, the Granville Public Market.

Though Vancouver, whose atmosphere is big-city like San Francisco's, hasn't a plethora of independent bed and breakfast inns (most are bed and breakfast homes), there will likely be more emerging for Expo 86.

FALSE CREEK BED & BREAKFAST

1124 Ironwork Passage
Vancouver, B.C. V6H 3P1
Owner/Innkeeper: Beryl Wilson
Telephone: (604) 734-3369
Rates: $30-$40

"I always encourage guests not to miss spending a day on Granville Island," says Beryl Wilson as we stand on the deck overlooking False Creek's colorful marina, which is filled with sailboats, tugboats, cabin cruisers, fishing boats, and even a canoe or two. Vancouver's downtown skyline is silhouetted against an orange and magenta sunset and the North Shore mountains, dark purple, beyond.

"I love it here on the water and the view is grand," she continues. "I do nearly all my shopping on the island [a tiny triangle five minutes away under the Granville Street Bridge] at the Granville Island Public Market. The locals go there, too."

Once an early Vancouver industrial area, Granville Island's old buildings have been spruced up without losing their original character and charm. Boats of every size and description fill the harbor, and the huge public market and shops for weavers, woodworkers, sculptors, and jewelry makers attract a lively trade. There are several good pubs and eateries, too.

At the public market Beryl finds cheeses, fresh-baked breads, croissants and bagels, fresh eggs and seasonal fruits, and special coffees and teas, which are transformed into delicious breakfast fare for her guests. On warm mornings enjoy eating your repast out on the patio or the seawall, taking advantage of the cityscapes and marine vistas.

Beryl offers travelers a comfortable queen-size bed in the guest room of her waterfront townhouse. The bath is shared, as are the living room, garden, patio, and laundry room. False Creek Bed and Breakfast is not suitable for children, but small pets may be permitted. "We are about 10 minutes from downtown Vancouver," explains Beryl, "and Expo 86 will be located nearby, just across False Creek."

GROUSE MOUNTAIN BED & BREAKFAST

900 Clements Avenue
North Vancouver, B.C. V7R 2K7
Owners/Innkeepers: Lyne & John Armstrong
Telephone: (604) 986-9630
Rates: $25-$35

"I'm just about ready to start my yearly ritual of jam making," explains Lyne when I phoned to ask about Grouse Mountain Bed and Breakfast. "I'm making blueberry, peach, strawberry, plum, raspberry, cherry, and blackberry. They're so popular with guests that several have suggested I sell it, but I prefer serving them with our full breakfast."

Lyne and John Armstrong have been plying bed and breakfast guests with their gourmet fruit preserves for about two years. Choose from two large pine-paneled guest rooms: one with a flagstone fireplace and rust carpeting, a small TV and an extra Chesterfield sofa-bed; the second, with cedar-paneled bath, has gold carpeting and warm accents.

Breakfast is ample and always accompanied by Lyne's jams and a very British pot of tea or coffee. The day might be warm enough for you to eat on one of two sun decks overlooking the rose garden where you can absorb views of nearby Grouse Mountain, Vancouver Island, and some of the Gulf Islands across the Strait of Georgia.

"We're just 10 minutes from Stanley Park," explains John. The park is an outdoor holiday with everything from jogging trails, tennis, and lawn bowling to a children's zoo, summer theatre, and aquarium. For a quiet walk, find tiny Beaver Lake, filled with lilies, pond grasses, and duck families–a peaceful spot to break away from the more crowded areas of the park.

HELEN ANN'S COTTAGE

1541 Ross Road
North Vancouver, B.C. V7J 1B7
Owners/Innkeepers: Helen & John Marshall
Telephone: (604) 980-0448
Rates: $25-$40

Located northeast of Burrard Inlet near Lynn Canyon Park, Helen Ann's Cottage offers a cozy retreat for travelers trekking to the future site of Expo 86.

Helen's guestroom–suite is done in cheerful chintz and country wallpaper with brass twin beds and an old-fashioned wicker chair. The private bath has a vintage mirror and is done in shades of brown with green and blue accents.

The sitting area, with its oak parquet floor, has a love seat and overstuffed chair, an 18th century armoire, a 50-year-old secretary, "with lots of books and magazines for browsing," adds Helen. "John is in the business of importing antiques from England, so we have some interesting old pieces of furniture."

Breakfast, served at an oval table in the dining room, "is wonderful and gourmet," says a fellow Vancouver innkeeper. Notice the Tiffany lamp, which sheds a warm glow on old china. Coffee arrives soon, or tea if you prefer, followed by a colorful fruit compote with a dollop of whipped cream, warm croissants with Helen's homemade jams, and perhaps a delicately poached egg nested in a carefully hollowed-out tomato. You may have to stay one more day so you can sample Helen's special blueberry pancakes.

KATIE'S BED & BREAKFAST

217 East Keith Road
North Vancouver, B.C. V7L 1V4
Owner/Innkeeper: Kathy Schmidt
Telephone: (604) 987-1092
Rates: $25-$35

Katie opened her large Victorian home, circa 1910, in North Vancouver to bed and breakfast guests in 1981. The original butler's anteroom has been transformed into a downstairs guest room, including a powder room and library with the original brass fireplace. Off the kitchen is a sunny breakfast area with a view of the water where guests meet for Katie's full breakfast.

On the second floor are two large suites with views of Burrard Inlet, Vancouver's inner harbour, and the downtown skyline. "Guests especially like the Roman bath with its blue tile tub and touches of elegance," says Katie.

A European-style common room with comfortable sitting places, fireplace, pillows, and books is an evening-by-the-fire gathering place for guests. "It's amazing how quickly people (from all corners of the world) become friends," she says.

Within seven blocks, on Lonsdale Avenue, is the Sea Bus terminal from which two 400-passenger ferries shuttle across Burrard Inlet to downtown Vancouver on trips that take about 10 minutes. It is one of the best on-water sightseeing bargains in town–smashing views of city and harbor for about 60 cents. Service runs from 6 a.m. to midnight.

NELLES' BED & BREAKFAST

1592 West 26th Avenue
Vancouver, B.C. V6J 2W9
Owners/Innkeepers: Gwen & Dick Nelles
Telephone: (604) 731-3556
Rates: $20-$35

"We live in one of the old tree-lined sections of Vancouver, the Shaughnessy district," explains Gwen. "It's almost like living in a park." The Nelles offer two airy and bright guest rooms on the second floor of their large family home.

"You won't find color-coordinated decorator linens and

plump goosedown comforters here," said Gwen, "but our guest rooms are clean and very comfortable with their wall-to-wall carpeting, good beds, and comfortable chairs. Travelers say how peaceful and quiet it is here."

"We like to think that we offer one of the best breakfasts in town," says Dick. Help yourself to two kinds of juice and fresh fruit set out on the buffet each morning. Perhaps you will be favored with Gwen's wild rice pancakes accompanied by blueberry sauce or maple syrup. Bacon and eggs–"the way you like them done"–and sausage, along with Gwen's hot bran muffins, are early morning favorites.

Nelles' Bed and Breakfast is close to downtown, the Granville Island Market, and Van Dusen Gardens, a botanical garden containing colorful plants, flowers, and shrubs from all over the world.

For travelers looking for warm Canadian hospitality in a family setting both comfortable and unpretentious, Nelles' Bed and Breakfast may just fit the itinerary.

ROSE GARDEN GUEST HOUSE

6808 Dawson Street
Vancouver, B.C. V5S 2W3
Owners/Innkeepers: Dwyla & Ed Beglaw
Telephone: (604) 435-7129
Rates: $25-$40

"Two years ago ours was chosen as one of the top ten gardens in the city by the *Vancouver Sun*," says Dwyla Beglaw. With more than 200 varieties of roses, including grandiflora, tea, floribunda, and miniatures, the Beglaws are proud to show off their prize-winning garden to bed and breakfast guests.

Dwyla harvests prime rose petals for drying and creates perfumed sachets, potpourri, scented pillows, and beribboned pictures using dried miniature roses. "Our guests enjoy them and many of the gift items are for sale," explains Dwyla.

Travelers find bright, clean guest rooms (one with handicap access) with a private entrance on the garden level. Baths are shared. One of the guest rooms has "old-fashioned Victorian-parlour ambience," to quote the innkeepers, with cozy love seat, overstuffed chair, desk, and double bed. A second guest room could accommodate a small family. "There is also a refrigerator on the porch for guests' use," says Dwyla.

Breakfast is wholesome at Rose Garden Guest House. Dwyla bakes whole-wheat muffins and biscuits, often containing almonds and sesame seeds, and serves up eggs with cheese accompanied by herbal teas and coffee. "We can also prepare a vegetarian breakfast of tofu scrambled eggs, if guests prefer," offer the Beglaws.

Rose Garden Guest House is located near Fraserview Golf Course, south of the downtown shopping area. The Beglaws recommend nearby Queen Elizabeth Park to garden lovers. The gardens, fashioned from two former stone quarries, are a flower-lover's delight. Enjoy as well the adjacent Bloedel Conservatory, a triodectic dome overflowing with orchids, anthurium, hibiscus and bright-feathered tropical birds. "The nearby Quarry House restaurant is a good lunch or dinner stop," says Dwyla.

For additional information (and maps) on what to see and do in Vancouver, contact: Greater Vancouver Visitors Bureau, Royal Centre Mall, 1055 West Georgia Street, P.O. Box 11142, Vancouver, B.C. V6E 4C8. Telephone: (604) 682-2222. Also: Southwestern British Columbia Tourist Association, P.O. Box 94449, Richmond, B.C. V6Y 2A8, Canada. For a list of bed and breakfast (home-stay style) reservation services, see list on page 132.

FERNHILL HERB FARM BED & BREAKFAST

P.O. Box 140
Fernhill Road
Mayne Island, B.C. V0N 2J0
Owners/Innkeepers: Brian & Mary Crumblehulme
Telephone: (604) 539-2544
Rates: $30-$40

"We decided to try a different lifestyle," explains Mary. "We visited several islands here and chose Mayne because we liked the rural feeling of it."

With several acres planted in culinary, fragrant, and medicinal herbs, Fernhill Herb Farm Bed and Breakfast comes by its name naturally. "We grow and sell fresh plants as well as the dried herbs," says Brian. From mugwort to lavender, thyme to garlic and basil, Brian and Mary's potpourri tour of the fragrant and pungent herb gardens offers guests a treat interesting and unique.

"We have two guest rooms with private baths for bed and breakfast travelers," says Mary. Antique buffs will enjoy the 17th century English antiques filling one suite with a Tudor four-poster, large Jacobean chest, dark wainscoting with off-white walls and maroon-and-cream comforter.

Guests who hanker for a rustic decor will enjoy the cedar-lined loft suite with its four-poster pine bed, brown quilt and matching curtains, and fresh daisy-patterned wallpaper.

"We invite our guests to gather around the wood stove in the lounge, play the piano, and browse through our collection of books," offer the Crumblehulmes. "We're just a ten-minute walk to the beach, a country store, or the local pub, and we can point out interesting historical spots to visit, too."

Breakfast, usually prepared by Brian, includes fresh eggs from the resident chickens, fresh-squeezed orange juice, and a large fruit plate. Mary bakes orange rolls or scones, "Something fresh every morning. We can also pack a picnic lunch and plan a dinner meal, on request."

Mayne Island, rural and friendly, is an easy ferry hop from Vancouver (or Vancouver Island). A good place to get away from the fast lane for awhile, unwind, soak in some silence–with an occasional cluck of a hen or crow of the family rooster to break your reverie. "The folks who have discovered us are sending their friends now," says Mary. "And that's the nicest compliment an innkeeper can receive."

CLIFFSIDE BED & BREAKFAST INN

General Delivery
Armadale Road
North Pender Island, B.C. V0N 2M0
Owner/Innkeeper: Penelope Tomlin
Telephone: (604) 629-6691
Rates: $35-$50

A short ferry ride from Vancouver will deposit travelers at Cliffside Bed and Breakfast Inn on North Pender Island. "We have some of the nicest beaches in all the Gulf Islands," says Penny, "and many lovely hidden coves for picnicking and sunning. Just last week I fixed cheeses and wine for guests who took a short climb to a nearby point–the view was supreme."

Cliffside Bed and Breakfast Inn is perched on 580 feet of oceanfront and has nearly a mile of beach to explore. "We have lots of clams and some oysters," explains Penny. "And our winter salmon fishing is excellent." Travelers may want to ask Penny about winter rates.

Available for guests' use are cod tackle and crab traps as well as two small boats. "Rowing to a nearby island with a picnic lunch is a favorite activity, too." How about a dinner cruise on a 45-foot ketch, *The Alstair,* or on a 35-foot motor cruiser? Penny can arrange either for a reasonable cost.

Relax in color-coordinated comfort with its nautical flair at Cliffside. The island property has been in Penny's family for over 50 years. Soft greys, whites, and blues are predominant colors, with fresh flowers, coordinated linens, and bath crystals in each of the four guest rooms. Water colors and oil paintings by local artists adorn the walls.

Enjoy the sundeck after a trek along the beach, contemplate your collected beach treasures, or just soak up salt air and seascapes–all 180 degrees of it at your disposal.

Breakfast? On cliff-hanger decks looking out on the Gulf Islands, with an abundance of fresh seafood, eggs, fruits, homemade breads, jams, tea and coffee–amid hanging flower baskets cascading with color. "I'll be offering an evening meal option this season," explains Penny, "with a choice of four different entrees, all made with fresh local products."

Penny promises bed and breakfast guests "a very mellow, friendly island experience. We also have space for a few tents (often fun for children) and tent trailers; these guests can enjoy a 'camper's special' breakfast for a small cost."

Cliffside Bed & Breakfast
N. Pender Island B.C.

A Bit of Old England . . .
Victoria

Swinging from old-fashioned blue lamp posts, Victoria's flower baskets spill over in reds, blues, whites, purples. Victoria is castles, totems, and museums. The Provincial Museum is a living history complete with sounds and aromas, and it is free. Victoria is afternoon tea, fish and chips, gourmet baked goods (try Dutch Bakery on Fort Street), fine dining, great shopping (Scottish tartans and English porcelain), and famous gardens (try the Butchart Gardens, about 15 miles north of downtown Victoria, created out of an old rock quarry).

Getting to Victoria is a pleasant experience for travelers because it involves water transportation to Vancouver Island. Take ferries from Seattle (*Princess Marguerite*), Anacortes (Washington State Ferries), Port Angeles (on the Hood Canal side, northwest of Port Townsend), and from Vancouver, B.C. (ferries leave from Tsawwassen, approximately 15 miles south of Vancouver, off Highway 99). For information call: Ministry of Transportation & Highways (604) 387-3996. For helpful information and city maps, contact: Greater Victoria Visitor Information Center, 812 Wharf Street (across from the Empress Hotel), Victoria, B.C. V8W 1T3. Telephone: (604) 382-2127.

BATTERY STREET GUEST HOUSE

670 Battery Street
Victoria, B.C. V8V 1E5
Owner/Innkeeper: Pamela Verduyn
Telephone: (604) 385-4632
Rates: $20-$40

If you want a functional, no-nonsense guest house close to Government Street, the Parliament buildings,

Museum, and Victoria harbor, the Battery Street Guest House may serve your needs.

The large, square house with its sun rooms on the front, "dates back to 1898," explains Pamela Verduyn. For some years it was a rest home, and in 1983 it opened as a downtown guest house. The guest rooms are located up one flight of stairs and are clean and functional in decor.

In a sunny breakfast porch, just beyond the common area, Pamela serves a continental breakfast at small tables that are usually decorated with flowers from her garden. Eat tasty orange or bran muffins, fresh fruit, juice, and coffee or tea.

"I like people," says Pamela with her slight Dutch accent, "and you meet such interesting people here in Victoria."

THE BEACONSFIELD INN

998 Humboldt Street
Victoria, B.C. V8V 2Z8
Owners/Innkeepers: Stuart Lloyd, Bill McKechnie
Telephone: (604) 384-4044
Rates: $50-$80

Travelers seeking an elegant, urban inn must add to their itinerary The Beaconsfield, Victoria's newest downtown bed and breakfast inn. It was built in 1905 by architect Samuel McClure for R.P. Rithet, as a wedding gift for Rithet's only daughter, Gertrude.

Gertrude married Lawrence Genge and lived in the house until her death in 1945. The Edwardian-English style house was later a home for the elderly. Following years of change and neglect, the house was purchased and reconstructed by Bill McKechnie, a lawyer turned developer.

Although painters were still on ladders when I visited, furniture and palms for the sunroom–conservatory had not arrived, and the smell of wallpaper paste permeated the air, it was obvious that The Beaconsfield would soon live up to its earlier tradition as home to a wealthy Victorian family.

The old English library on the main floor contains dark leather sofas, red oriental rug, the original mantled fireplace, and floor-to-ceiling bookshelves filled with austere reading material. "Most of the shelves and woodwork are the original," explains Bill McKechnie. "We found them under the house."

Each of the guest rooms has a descriptive name, such as The Blue Room and The Verandah Room, or is named for a person in history. The Oscar Room takes its name from Oscar Wilde, and its colors from his favored lavender. The Lillie Room is named after Edward VII's mistress, Lillie Langtry.

The Beaconsfield Inn was named after a posh London hotel frequented by King Edward VII (he and Lillie met there for their romantic liaisons, away from the disapproving Queen Victoria and Edward's wife, Alexandra) during his reign in pre-World War I England.

"The original McClure plans were found with the help of an historian at the University of Victoria's archives," explains Bill. "They were very helpful, and now the house has been declared a Heritage Building by the City of Victoria and is on the National Inventory of Historic Buildings.

"Otherwise, the house would probably have been torn down to make way for an asphalt parking lot or something equally unpleasing," adds Stuart.

You might imagine that breakfast at The Beaconsfield would be served in a formal dining room beneath old crystal chandeliers, but it isn't. Guests are invited to gather at the long oval table in the light, airy kitchen for fresh fruit, an omelette, bacon or sausages, homemade scones, jams, and fresh brewed coffee.

"Seeing some of these large 19th-century homes transformed from neglect to urban and rural bed and breakfast inns is exciting," says Stuart. "It seems a more fitting destiny than the wrecker's ball."

CAMPUS VIEW BED & BREAKFAST

1840 Midgard Avenue
Victoria, B.C. V8P 2Y9
Owners/Innkeepers: Elsie & Don Laird
Telephone: (604) 477-3069
Rates: $25-$39

"I'll never forget the time Don took our pickup out along Elk Lake in a pouring rainstorm to pick up guests who were touring on bicycles," smiles Elsie. "A couple with a small child; we got everyone into warm clothes and fixed a pot of tea."

You will find this brand of hospitality in most bed and breakfast homes like the Lairds, who offer refurbished, clean guest rooms on the second floor of their suburban home near the University of Victoria, about 10 minutes from downtown.

Bed and breakfast guests are invited to become part of the Laird family and have the use of the family living room, dining room, and sun porch. "We offer both comfort and security," explains Elsie. "We have hosted visiting lecturers from the Weavers Guild, kayakers from New Brunswick, as well as single women and traveling salesmen."

Breakfast is a sumptuous affair at the family dining room table–fresh fruit compote, sliced tomatoes, eggs or sometimes a quiche, bacon, hash browns, homemade jam, and tea.

ELK LAKE BED & BREAKFAST

5259 Pat Bay Highway
Victoria, B.C. V8Y 1S8
Owners/Innkeepers: Elaine & Frank Devine
Telephone: (604) 658-8879
Rates: $38-$40

We are sitting in the comfortable and inviting common room sampling Elaine's mouth-watering apple pie and sipping tea. Sofas and chairs are in conversational groupings in the large room; I see polished coffee tables, a well-loved recliner in front of the TV, mantled fireplace, an antique upright piano. The room is large enough to hold a fair-sized congregation of people.

"Actually, the house used to be a church," explains Elaine. Small leaded-and-stained-glass windows encircle the common room, the former sanctuary, at ceiling level, admitting warm light. The room is filled with antiques from Ireland and Scotland–see the lovely collection of Belleek and the library full of classics.

Walk two steps up to the dining alcove, which is dominated by a formal antique table with matching high-backed carved chairs. Lace curtains, built-in oak china cupboard, polished wood wainscoting, and crystal chandelier set the mood for Elaine's breakfast.

"I usually serve orange juice, homemade Scotch sausage, Irish soda bread, pancakes, and fresh fruit," says Elaine. "My guests seem to develop large appetites when they stay here."

There are four guest rooms–two on the main level and two on the second floor, up a narrow stairway that may have led to a bell tower or pastoral study-suite. You'll find old-fashioned lavender sachet bags on your stack of towels, along with chestnuts and bay leaves in the closets–"a sure thing for keeping wee spiders away," winks Elaine.

HERITAGE HOUSE BED & BREAKFAST

1100 Burnside Road West
Victoria, B.C. V8Z 1N3
Owners/Innkeepers: Irvin & Doreen Stang
Telepone: (604) 479-0892
Rates: $29-$35

"Why don't you come on out, we would like you to see our place," says Irvin cordially over the phone. I nearly miss the small sign and driveway as I drive from downtown Victoria toward the Saanich area, about 10 minutes from downtown.

"People are always surprised to find such a big place set back so far from the road in the trees," explains Doreen. Set amid two acres beautifully landscaped and maintained by Irvin, Heritage House is a petite mansion dating back to the early 1900s. The Stangs discovered the house in disrepair on a trip from Alberta, where Irvin owned a trucking firm, bought it, and moved from the prairie country to Vancouver Island. "We love it here," says Doreen. "Especially the mild winters."

On the second floor are three large guest rooms with shared bath, decorated with family antiques and warm

High Tea —
A tradition in Victoria
Heritage House

colors. One guest room has a private balcony overlooking the front gardens, rolling lawn, and curved drive. Another has a brass bed, yellow floral-print wallpaper, yellow tie-back curtains, and a white wicker settee. A large foyer adjoining the guest rooms serves as a comfortable lounge and has a small TV for guests' use.

Doreen prepares breakfast in her large country kitchen with its own pot-bellied wood stove. Nearby the two family dachshunds usually reside. Your breakfast of eggs, bacon, toast, and homemade jams and jellies is served in the wood-panelled Victorian dining room on antique china. Notice the built-in sideboard and china cupboard with old, leaded glass windows.

"We encourage guests to use the garden and front porch with its table and deck chairs," says Doreen "though most people are off exploring Victoria during the day. Irvin and I try out different restaurants and tea rooms so that we can recommend places to our guests."

One of Victoria's time-honored traditions is afternoon tea, usually served from two to five at various hotels and intimate tearooms throughout the city. "You'll find yourself a firm believer within two or three days," says Doreen with a smile.

In Victoria, you'll find an authentic English tea heritage (it evolved in the late 1700s among aristocracy as an elaborate snack to sustain them until supper at 8 p.m.). Shops owned or operated by Britons carry a colorful array of tea cozies, hand-painted cups, and silver services. Afternoon tea menus include raisin scones, cheese crumpets, fruit buns, dainty sandwiches, fresh fruit and fruit trifles, and often a rich and delicious imitation of Devonshire clotted cream.

You may not equal the daily intake of Samuel Johnson, who called himself a "hardened and shameless tea drinker" (he was said to have consumed 30 to 40 cups a day) but, like most Victorians, bed and breakfast travelers may enjoy indulging in "a cuppa" during their excursion to this bit of old England named for one of her queens. Find a complete list of tearooms at the visitors center on Wharf Street across from the Empress.

OAK BAY GUEST HOUSE

1052 Newport
Victoria, B.C. V8S 5E3
Owners/innkeepers: Bryan & Joan Savage
Telephone: (604) 598-3812
Rates: $28-$40

Located in an old, elegant neighborhood near Oak Bay, the Oak Bay Guest House offers eleven rooms with private baths in the British tradition.

"When the Oak Bay Hotel (nearby) occasionally sends travelers here," says innkeeper Bryan Savage, "I ask them to remind people that we're not a hotel; our guest rooms don't have telephones or TV, and we don't have valet and room service. Being waited on 'hand and foot' isn't usually possible in a smaller, more intimate inn. It's a more casual and sociable way of traveling, like the bed and breakfast inns in England, Scotland, or Europe."

Bed and breakfast innkeepers wear many hats–"we often do our own baking and grocery shopping, our own yard work and maintenance and cleaning, as well as answering the telephone and making reservations. And meeting guests with a friendly welcome."

Most travelers agree that the benefits of this mode of travel far outweigh not having room service, telephones or television. "Where else can you sleep in carved, antique four-posters or elegant brass-and-iron with bona fide down comforters and linens in matching decorator colors," says one bed and breakfast guest. "With fresh flowers on the antique nightstand or chest of drawers, live plants everywhere, books and magazines from the family library, and those waist-bulging breakfasts."

Breakfast at Oak Bay Guest House is sustaining fare served from 8 to 9 each morning. Coffee from the local gourmet coffee company and Joan's homemade marmalade and jams are special treats.

At the far corner of the second floor is a large sun porch filled with plants, sofa, books, game table, and small TV for guests' use. Nearby is Monterey Mews, with courtyard shops in an English Tudor setting. "Also nearby are the Sea Gardens, a marina, golf course, library, and city buses," explain Joan and Bryan.

ROSE COTTAGE BED & BREAKFAST

3059 Washington Avenue
Victoria, B.C. V9A 1P7
Owner/Innkeeper: Linda Simpson
Telephone: (604) 381-5985
Rates: $25-$35 (flexible)

"Rose Cottage is probably one of the smallest European-style inns in the area," says Linda Simpson with a smile. We sit at the kitchen table sipping tea and eating ginger cookies.

The light blue, Victorian-style house, circa 1912, is in a family neighborhood about two miles from downtown Victoria. "Megan [age five] and I enjoy people, and children are especially welcome here," says Linda. "We can also arrange for childcare."

Guests at Rose Cottage come downstairs from functional, pleasant guest rooms with shared bath to the formal dining room for a four-course breakfast served on English bone china, pewter, and silver. Linda may have on hand her special homemade preserves–rhubarb jam, marmalade, blackberry-apple or crabapple jelly. They all go well with crumpets, pancakes, and scones. "I enjoy cooking for people who enjoy eating," says Linda.

If you're planning a day of seeing the sights of Victoria, browse through the large selection of brochures and information displayed on the nearby sideboard. The comfortable living room with its oak-mantled, coal-burning fireplace is also for guests' use, as is the library wall in the dining room.

Well-traveled, Linda managed hotels and traveled the bed and breakfast route in Scotland for five years. "Our guests range from far and wide; a couple from Ireland, students from Europe, lawyers from England."

I leave, taking the ginger cookie Linda wraps in a napkin for me. "That's what hospitality is all about," she smiles. "When you have a guest who comes in weary from traveling, even at 11 p.m., you offer them a cup of tea and perhaps a scone, along with a warm welcome." When I think of scones, I remember a small tearoom near the Parliament buildings, a warm morning in May, and tea served in the English-Scottish tradition–piping hot and accompanied by raisin scones, slathered with butter and jam.

For information, maps, and brochures describing things to see and do in Victoria and on Vancouver Island, contact: Greater Victoria Visitors Center, 812 Wharf Street, Victoria, B.C. V8W 1T3. Telephone: (604) 382-2127. Travelers looking for the bed and breakfast home-type accommodation in the Victoria area will find a list of reservation services on page 133.

A Sampling . . .

SE Alaska, Montana

Voss Inn

THE VOSS INN

319 South Willson Street
Bozeman, MT 59715
Owners/Innkeepers: Ruthmary & Ken Tonn
and Voss
Telephone: (406) 587-0982
Rates: $45-$55

In 101 years, the rambling, two-story Victorian mansion changed from a single-family dwelling to a home for apartment dwellers to a haven for bed and breakfast travelers passing through Bozeman.

The house was built in 1883 for Frank A. Armstrong, a district attorney, who was also a state legislator and speaker of the House in 1887. "In 1890 the house was bought by a former Civil War colonel, O. P. Chisholm, who moved here from Illinois to practice law and run the county land office," explains Ruthmary.

The Voss Inn, of red brick with Victorian gingerbread porches on each side, is located on a tree-lined street between downtown Bozeman and the Montana State University campus. Each of the six guest rooms has a private bath and a special name and personality. New floral wallpapers, old-fashioned, brass-and-iron beds, polished wood floors, oriental rugs, tables, reading lamps, and white curtains help convey a Victorian-era ambiance.

Relax in the elegant parlor and get acquainted. "The inn allows us to live in a beautiful old home and meet people from all over the world," say the Tonns. A piano, antique oak Victrola, color TV, selection of books and magazines, a chess set, and cards are available for guests' use.

For breakfast, trek to the hutch in the upstairs hall, beginning about 6:30 a.m., and serve yourself coffee and homemade cinnamon rolls kept hot in an ornate 1880s bun-warmer in the radiator. Then help yourself to an individual egg-cheese-ham souffle. "It's nice to spend your day doing something that makes travelers feel comfortable," says Ruthmary.

EXCELSIOR HOUSE

319 North Excelsior Street
Butte, MT 59701
Owner/Innkeeper: Sarah Wyss
Telephone: (406) 723-7905
Rates: $20-$35

"The double bay windows with stained glass and the two fireplaces in the living room always intrigue our visitors," says innkeeper Sarah Wyss. Built in 1895, Excelsior House is surrounded by ostentatious turn-of-the-century homes of legendary copper kings and miners. "Butte is so full of history," says Sarah. "It makes you want to drop everything and spend weeks in the historic museum and archives reading old letters and looking at old photographs."

Bed and Breakfast travelers have six guest rooms with shared baths in which to rest weary bones, each renovated and redecorated in Victorian splendor by Sarah. "I enjoy collecting vintage clothing, too," she says. "Guests are welcome to look at gowns and outfits – some are for sale."

Sarah offers a substantial breakfast of small pastries, Povitica, quiches, sourdough bread or baking powder biscuits, plus an array of fresh fruits and coffee. Enough to fortify visitors for a day of energetic sight-seeing in historic Butte.

Be sure to include on your itinerary the Copper King Mansion, with its 32 rooms, including a 62-foot ballroom and a pipe organ. And there is the World Museum of Mining, with its indoor and outdoor mining exhibits, as well as Hell Roarin' Gulch, a restored 1900s mining camp with Chinese laundry, an assay office, a sauerkraut factory, and ladies millinery shop.

If your feet are in good shape (Butte is built on a hillside), try a walking tour of historic Uptown Butte, using the historical society's self-guided map describing about 40 historic homes, businesses, and community buildings.

"You'll recognize Excelsior House," says Sarah. "It's the one with the double bay windows repainted in four vintage Victorian colors."

GUSTAVUS INN

P.O. Box 31
Gustavus, AK 99826
Owners/Innkeepers: David & JoAnn Lesh
Telephone: (907) 697-3311 (summer)
(907) 586-2006 (winter)
Rates: $75 (per adult, per day)
$55 (per child, per day)

"People who don't like fish will eat our fish, and folks who don't eat breakfast will eat our breakfast," teases JoAnn Lesh. Come mornings at Gustavus Inn, chief cook David Lesh opens the sourdough pot for pancakes (the huge, golden, fluffy kind) and piles heaps of eggs and bacon on guests' plates along with wild berry jam and rhubarb preserves.

Most items on the Gustavus Inn table are from the sea, the sourdough pot, or the large summer garden. The smell of baking bread is an aromatic happening daily. Because of its isolated location east of Juneau, chef Lesh serves three meals a day which are included in the cost per person. Lunches and dinners feature fresh garden soups, salads, vegetables, and local fish (dungeness crab, king salmon, silver salmon, halibut and trout), with a sourdough or whole-grain bread and a crock of seaweed pickles to complement the lots. Plus dessert . . . maybe a rhubarb sherbet or chocolate whiskey cake.

Gustavus Inn was founded as a farm in 1928 and is maintained in that tradition by David and JoAnn Lesh. Dave's parents, Sally and Jack Lesh, launched the inn some 18 years ago, homesteading from the East Coast in a school bus with four children.

Seven rooms are freshly refurbished in an attached quonset hut, with shared baths. Most rooms have twin beds; a few have double beds. Paintings by Alaska artists and historic photographs of the area are tacked to hallway walls.

There's a cozy Alaskan library and a six-stool pub. Until 1975 the inn had the only telephone in Gustavus, and the post office once resided in the backyard shed.

A fleet of blue bicycles are available for guests. Bike down flat gravel roads to Icy Straits (about two miles) with a picnic lunch. Everyone waves; no exceptions, and "it's the only obstacle to road safety," laughs Dave. Gawk at hip-high blue and purple lupine or shoulder-high white-cow turnips. Or the 25-foot tides. Or Fairweather mountain range–"it appears now and then on its own schedule, unknown to the rest of us." Another short trip just down the road is to the Wannigan, Sally Lesh's weaving studio (the shelter was once a floating brothel for the salmon fleet). She grows the wool, spins it, and dyes it with vegetable dyes from wildflowers.

Where is Gustavus, travelers ask? It's located west of Juneau about 50 miles as the crow flies, a settlement at the gateway to Glacier Bay and Glacier Bay National Park and Preserve. Guests are welcome from May through September. Do not try to drive to Gustavus; there are no roads leading there yet. You can fly in on Alaska Airlines, and the Leshs will pick you up at the Gustavus runway where World War II planes used to land.

"Bring your outdoor clothes and gear," suggests JoAnn. "We don't use much formal wear up here." Who would mind, with bouquets of wildflowers on the table and platters of fresh dungeness crab and king salmon sitting on checkered tablecloths.

For information about the area contact: Alaska Natural History Association, Glacier Bay National Monument,

Gustavus, AK 99826 (publications, maps, hiking trails, etc.), and Southeast Alaska Tourism Council, P.O. Box 7055-DT, Ketchikan, AK 99901. Telephone: (907) 225-6167.

Reservation Services . . .

Bed & Breakfast Homes

Northwest Bed and Breakfast
7707 S.W. Locust Street
Portland, OR 97223
(503) 246-8366

PT International
1318 S.W. Troy Street
Portland, OR 97219
(503) 245-0440 or (800) 547-1463

Pacific Bed and Breakfast
701 N.W. 60th Street
Seattle, WA 98107
(206) 784-0539

Traveller's Bed and Breakfast
P.O. Box 492
Mercer Island, WA 98040
(206) 232-2345

Babs
P.O. Box 5025
Bellingham, WA 98227
(206) 733-8642

Spokane Bed and Breakfast
P.O. Box 11103
Spokane, WA 99211
(509) 924-9229
(509) 924-0840

Panorama Land Bed and Breakfast
117 West Astor Street
Colville, WA 99114
(509) 684-4571

Canadian Bed and Breakfast
Victoria (604) 381-3312
Vancouver: (604) 321-1265

Olde Victoria Bed and Breakfast Registry
P.O. Box 5083, Station 'B'
Victoria, B.C. V8R 6N3
(604) 592-5038

Victoria Bed and Breakfast Inc.
209-703 Broughton
Victoria, B.C. V8W 1E2
(604) 385-2332

VIP Bed and Breakfast
1786 Teakwood Road
Victoria, B.C. V8N 1E2
(604) 477-5604

Born Free Bed and Breakfast Agency
4390 Frances Street
Burnaby, B.C. V5C 2R3
(604) 298-8815

The Old English Bed and Breakfast Registry
363 East 8th Street
North Vancouver, B.C. V7L 1Z2
(604) 986-5069
(604) 943-8241

Alaska Bed and Breakfast Association
526 Seward Street-DT
Juneau, AK 99801
(907) 586-2959

Alaska Private Lodgings
Box 110135-DT
Anchorage, AK 99511
(907) 345-2222

Fairbanks Bed and Breakfast
Box 74573
Fairbanks, AK 99707
(907) 452-4967